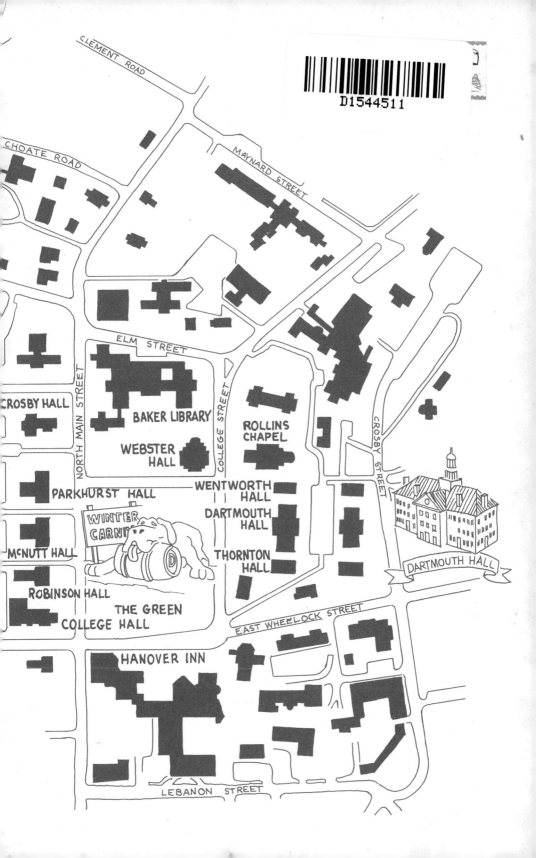

CLEMENT ROAD

CHOATE ROAD

MAYNARD STREET

ELM STREET

NORTH MAIN STREET

COLLEGE STREET

CROSBY STREET

CROSBY HALL

BAKER LIBRARY

WEBSTER HALL

ROLLINS CHAPEL

PARKHURST HALL

WENTWORTH HALL

DARTMOUTH HALL

WINTER CARN

MCNUTT HALL

THORNTON HALL

DARTMOUTH HALL

ROBINSON HALL

THE GREEN

COLLEGE HALL

EAST WHEELOCK STREET

HANOVER INN

LEBANON STREET

It's Different at DARTMOUTH

Jean Alexander Kemeny

It's Different at
DARTMOUTH

A MEMOIR BY

Jean Alexander Kemeny

THE STEPHEN GREENE PRESS
BRATTLEBORO, VERMONT

*This book has been produced in the United States of
America: It is designed by Robert R. Anderson, and published by The Stephen Greene Press, Brattleboro, Vermont
05301*

LIBRARY OF CONGRESS CATALOGING IN PUBLICATION DATA
Kemeny, Jean Alexander, 1930–
   It's different at Dartmouth.

   1. Dartmouth College—History. 2. Dartmouth
College—Miscellanea. I. Title.
LD1438.K45   378.742'3   79–18030
ISBN 0–8289–0358–1

Dedicated to
the Thirteenth President
of Dartmouth College

Contents

A section of photographs follows page 110.

The book endpapers show a partial map of Dartmouth College

Acknowledgments

ALL THESE PEOPLE helped: Maurice Rapf, Marian Searchinger and Mary Yost, Chas Carner, Lu and John Sterling, Mona Chamberlin, Kathy Tefft, Denise Alexander, the group at The Stephen Greene Press, Phoebe Killham, Betty Shepard, Alex Fanelli, Elaine O'Brien, Margot de L'Etoile and others I may have inadvertently forgotten to mention.

Recognition and special thanks go to: Ruth La Bombard, who solved a myriad of problems; Dick Hansen, who set me on the right track; Mrs. James Bryant Conant, who gave time and much of herself. She was to be and deserved a chapter, but because the focus of the book changed, her contribution shows up only indirectly. Thanks also to Bea Jones, who transcribed and typed the early drafts, and Deborah O'Loughlin, who typed and retyped the final drafts, sometimes trekking from Concord to make deadlines; Nancy Wasserman, who took a large number of photographs, of which only a few appear here; Bill Eastman, my editor, who had perception and patience; Sue Prindle, who copy edited with empathy and humor; my mother and father, Laura Philbrick Bliss and Robert Burton Alexander, who taught me that language, living and people are important; Jenny and Rob Kemeny, two children who endured their life in the President's House and enriched ours; and my husband, who prodded me when I procrastinated, who organized me when I flew off in all directions and who offered constructive criticism when I was ready to destruct the whole project. He was always there.

Preface

WHEN I was sixteen and watched my great-aunt, whose husband was Master of Silliman College at Yale, go into action entertaining and running a large, imposing house, I knew what I did *not* want to be when I grew up. A cowed country mouse, I watched with awe as my aunt rushed enthusiastically into battle with the force of a Panzer division.

I grew up and became a professor's wife. I *still* knew what I would be lousy at—playing a major public role. As a hostess I was hopeless. I gave only three small dinners a year, but I agonized over each ordeal for weeks.

So what have I become? The wife of the President of Dartmouth! Entertaining and running a large house are only one facet of my job—but that facet is larger than my great-aunt's job! What prepared me for this role? Awkwardness, insecurity and terror.

"And what do *you* do, Mrs. Kemeny?" is a common question —cooed cattily by a few and asked seriously by hundreds. The job is complex. By the time I finished answering, dawn would be breaking.

It seemed easier to write a book about the job. Dash something off and answer every conceivable question. What an innocent! I couldn't dash: I plodded, meandered in circles, backtracked a lot and plopped down to catch my breath. A novice, I didn't understand about time—that writers need blocs of it: peaceful periods to plot and organize, uncluttered time to contemplate and create.

Uncluttered time? What's that? I scribbled notes when not much else was happening (3 AM seemed safe). I noted under hair dryers, in terminals, on buses and in airplanes—when I wasn't gripping the armrests.

I collected *almost* all the notes. Those that are missing are surely safe, for I hid them. (Where, I have no idea.) Some notes had to be discarded: the ones that were hastily scribbled on handy paper towels—ink bleeds; also those precious pieces of paper which an escaping cat assumed were there for his use only—ink runs; and those notes that a gust of wind blew into a chlorinated pool—ink dissolves.

What remained had to be organized. I needed space, lots of it. The dining-room table was appropriated. I spread out my now neatly organized folders, set up a typewriter and began. Immediately we had a dinner party. I grabbed a smaller table. Hors d'oeuvres for a cocktail party took precedence. I moved to the kitchen table, and amidst commotion and chatter and cats in my lap, I tried. Overcoming all hazards, I finished a very rough first draft—a sometimes silly, sometimes serious, sometimes satirical view of my life as first lady of Dartmouth—only to discover that ladies weren't selling. "Is it a book on women's lib?" (No, but it's *Totally* different from Marabel's *Woman.*) "How much anger is in it?" (Some honest fury, little anger.) "Well, does it have *any* sex?!" (Damn—I didn't recount orgies or count orgasms!)

Should I reassess the situation? Should I write a *roman à clef* or a "nonfiction" novel reeking of introspection and self-analysis, since that seems to be the rage? If the public scrambles to buy a book which vomits up every sordid detail, why not? Confession is catharsis, however contrived. And, after all, there's hardly a reviewer extant who won't gush over anything that purports to delve into a woman's psyche (and has shock value).

If shocking revelations are in vogue, I'll use my recipe for the perfect potboiler:

Set the pot on simmer. Throw in exotic sexual facts or fantasies—the more, the better. Add a touch of bisexuality, a whiplash of sadism, and lace with alcohol. Pop in some pills and a pinch of coke, crush in a handful of bitter herbs and sprinkle over with angel dust. Turn up the heat to boil. Bruise a few sensitive nerve endings and add them. Measure out a lifetime of rejection, stir up several times and then add two nervous breakdowns and one suicide attempt. Plop in a dollop of male abuse and beat briskly. Tear the flesh from the still quivering carcass, chop and grind to a pulp. Toss in with the bare bones. Season to taste with any leftover masochism and then stew.

What an unappetizing recipe! I can't swallow the dish. Back to a less spicy first draft, but truth does not have to be bland.

The first draft is accepted, if I revise. (The first draft *was* sloppy.) The second draft is torn apart (by me) and penciled out (by my editor), cut, reorganized and rewritten into the third draft. But that needs work; my standards are rising. Are we now at the fourth draft? (Why did I ever mention to *anybody* that I was writing a book? I could have quit quietly.) I complain that I *must* have uninterrupted time, until a friend points out that if I had enough time to write, there wouldn't be anything to write about! The fourth draft reads well—to me. Why are the sacred paragraphs marked up? Why are those incisive thoughts questioned? (To the editor: *I* thought my sentence in the ninth chapter was pretty damn funny!) The fifth draft is it. I have no more strength and my typewriter is wearing thin. Cut-off time has come. No more tidbits. If tomorrow, I should be asked to be United States Chief of Protocol, I would not add the honor. But not to worry; I'm last on *that* list.

Here it is. My portrait of an institution to which I have a very special relationship. Wives of public figures have written at length about their lives; wives of university presidents have said little. Oh, they've been quoted in interviews, some statistical surveys have been taken about their common problems and there are a few books written in an earlier, much more simple age, pastorally charming and dated.

This book is a memoir, an anecdotal account of my life as a college president's wife. It is the story of a job that is ill defined and barely understood. I detail the stimulation, excitement and frustration of a role that I have structured myself. Perhaps I am atypical of the breed, for it *is* different at Dartmouth.

It's Different at DARTMOUTH

How Did I Get Here?

THE STOCK MARKET crashed with a bang in 1929, and the Depression began. I came into the world exactly a year later with a whimper—depressed, no doubt, because my birth was not taken seriously. During labor, my father and the obstetrician did not pace; they sat on the bottom of my mother's hospital bed, pitching cards into a hat perched on her bulging belly—on me! Vermonters were not easily impressed by natural events. In a state which had more cows than people, veterinarians and calves were more revered than M.D.'s and babies. Calves were cash money.

We left Burlington a month later when my father, a young insurance agent with New York Life, was transferred to Maine. I grew up on the coast in Cape Elizabeth where there are more rocks than people. Rocks don't reproduce, but they are picturesque and do hold the sea back. Until I went to college, I lived 100 feet from that sea.

Cape Elizabeth was only beginning to be a bedroom town for Portland, so many of the children in the tiny school were from Coast Guard or Merchant Marine families; others had fathers and brothers who went out daily in small lobster and fishing boats. The sea dominated our lives. It provided jobs, fed us and killed us. Magnificent when raging in a hurricane, tranquilly deceptive on a glittering Summer's day, it is schizophrenic, cruel and untrustworthy.

My parents, both Vermonters, were caught by the sea; they

grew to love it more than the hills in which they had been bred.

Alexander's Drug Store is still in St. Albans. As a child Daddy worked for his father behind the soda counter or wrapping prescriptions. Somehow all five boys graduated from college. Daddy, fatherless at twelve, paid his way through Yale waiting on table, working as a cowboy one Summer in the Canadian Rockies and selling his blood as often as possible. (Some of that blood money bought out-of-season violets for my mother.)

At Yale he excelled in athletics; later he would teach his two daughters the things boys did, but girls did not. A warm, outgoing man, he lights up a room. He was (and still is) a marvelous father.

When she was young, my mother was usually missing. "Laura is off reading!" Rheumatic fever limited her outdoor activities (she always said that clock golf was her most strenuous sport), so she began to write. She graduated Phi Beta Kappa from the University of Vermont in her hometown of Burlington. Her honors thesis on identical twins was still being referred to by professors at Harvard a decade ago.

She should have been an officer in the Baker Street Irregulars. To her, Sherlock Holmes lived. She did double-crostics ruthlessly—*nothing* could be looked up. She also knitted ruthlessly —miserable things like argyle socks with all those dangling bobbins, while simultaneously reading a book and carrying on a coherent conversation. She wrote beautifully, prose and poetry reminiscent of Phyllis McGinley. Her great desire was to crack *The New Yorker*. She never did. She died too young from heart surgery.

A picture of me at four shows a sweet-faced child with golden curls. That blond angel hid a devil plotting to get rid of an intruder—a baby sister. I tried to starve her by stealing her bottles. When that failed, I bossed her, and when she was old enough to fight, we did, constantly.

Judy got even. There was a period when I wouldn't walk downtown with her—a ten-year-old with a pixie sense of humor. She could embarrass me with a twitch. And twitch she did, contorting her face, jerking her arms and legs weirdly. I'd run ahead. (I don't know you!)

But I am rather proud of her. Her acting ability increased. At sixteen she was in summer stock in Ogunquit, getting better reviews than Kay Francis. She went on to Antioch briefly, married, had three children and then went back to college. She stuck out eight years, got her degree and now has had several successful shows as an artist. Her determination would not have been nearly as strong if she hadn't had me for an older sister!

We were hit hard by the Depression. People were scrimping to buy food, not insurance. Yet during the thirties we had a maid—a live-in teenager, paid $5 a week.

Judy and I believed in Santa Clause longer than most children, for we heard him. Daddy jumped down through the skylight on the roof, then clumped down the stairs, ho-ho-ho-ing. We shook in our beds. Very solemnly he told us that at midnight on Christmas Eve all the animals could talk, and we believed. The year I recognized the handwriting on the thank-you note for a snack we had left, Santa Claus became a myth. But I still have faith in the animals.

The family played hide-and-seek when we were little. I remember crouching under the laundry in the clothes hamper. But the best hiding place (my mother had to give up) was high up on a cupboard shelf *behind* all the canned goods.

Both of us inherited our father's talent for amateur acting. When he played Old Muff Potter in *Tom Sawyer,* we cried. "Daddy's in jail!" We recovered when the bars began to wobble. Rubber! Any fool could escape.

My mother believed that certain things were "done." Therefore, I was sent to dancing school at age eight. I rather liked my blue velvet dress with the lace collar; I tolerated the Mary Janes which cracked; I despised the classes, stiff and formal. I was too tall and couldn't dance. The boys were too short and couldn't dance. I still can't dance.

Sunday school was also "done." Judy and I, normally noisy during the week, were exceptionally quiet on the seventh day. We rested—on top of the piano—and prayed that our parents would oversleep. Another dreary lesson missed! I rarely go to church now.

Books: I devoured them. The house was filled with them. I

read in every conceivable place and after hours with a flashlight under the covers. Before I was ten, I could switch easily from *The Blue Fairy Book* to *The New Yorker* or *Legal Medicine and Toxicology* (covering up the more gruesome pictures). I treasured the *Oz* books, *Poor Little Rich Girl* and bound copies of *St. Nicholas*. And Agatha Christie—it's unfortunate that I began with *The Murder of Roger Ackroyd*.

Blackout curtains, rationing and victory gardens meant war. But the Second World War was closer to those of us on the coast. We saw it and heard it. The *Yorktown* sailed past our house before Midway. Soldiers and dogs patrolled the beach in front of the house. Submarine nets strung underwater protected the entrance to Portland Harbor; planes flew over the house every morning on dawn patrol, circling and searching for U-boats; we heard depth charges launched during daylight and saw the flash of rockets fired in the darkness; and we picked up things on the beach—waterlogged lifebelts, naval caps—flotsam from freighters sunk by the U-boats.

My first Summer job was infamous. With the country at war, there were no men to cultivate the crops in the truck-gardens, so they were hiring anyone—including a thirteen-year-old girl. Up before 6 AM to be in the fields by 7, I weeded carrots exclusively. The only bright spot was the group of Jamaicans imported to help. I had never met a black person before. They sang all day and kept our spirits up. By 10 AM I was starving and snitched carrots from the ground, devouring them, dirt and all. My pay was 35 cents an hour. I did not last the Summer.

I played the bass viol, an instrument which looks like a violin with thyroid problems. Its strings are taut and heavy enough to moor a supertanker and should be manipulated only by a stevedore. When played well, the bass viol has a certain dignified tone. When played badly, it grunts. As a high-school freshman, I played it abominably. The two requirements—a tall person who would not move away—fit me to a T. I maneuvered that bulky thing on and off the school bus to rehearsals which I disrupted. While the orchestra played merrily, I bowed mournful groans at odd times. I did not last the Fall.

My father is a rock hound and gives lectures on minerals to grade schools. When they were first married, Mummy would go with him on "pick and shovel" expeditions. But physical exercise was hard on her, so gradually Judy and I would do outdoor things with Daddy. We were company to him, we had fun and we learned.

He was ahead of his time. We went jogging thirty years before it became a fad; thirty years before 500 books were written on the subject and 50 million fanatics were clogging up the highways trying to unclog their arteries. We jogged in the dark on freezing winter mornings over rocky beaches covered with ice and snow. We slithered and fell and finally quit. I shall not jog again.

We skated for miles on an inland river which flowed to the sea. We skied, even going to Stowe before it was a jet-set resort —and before I had modern equipment. Snowplowing the Toll Road—four miles of pure ice—with antique bindings and no edges, put me in a crouched position for twenty-four hours. We climbed—to the top of the roof. We fished from the rocks in front of the house with a bamboo pole, periwinkle bait and a stout rope to tie us to those rocks. One slip and out to sea with the undertow. We caught bony cunner, which tastes like perch, and sculpin—inedible, frightening sea monsters.

I had my own rifle, a Marlin rimfire .32, my grandfather's squirrel gun. I was a good shot on tin cans, but I never aimed at animals. I could take that rifle apart and put it back together blindfolded.

Tennis? There was only one court in town, and that belonged to an estate. I never learned. Golf? I associate golf courses with a massive case of poison ivy and stay off them. Baseball? I had hitting talent, and I could side-arm ground balls—unpredictable grounders with spin and hop to them. I was in great demand among high-school boys trying out for the infield. I was baseball crazy; the Red Sox were my team and I was in love with them all. Master actors, those announcers who did the play-by-play from Western Union ticker tape. I didn't keep a diary; I kept a score card, recording every play of every game.

I could rattle off each player's stats, including put-outs and assists. And when, in 1947, an all-Maine baseball clinic was held for high-school youths, I went too. (Johnny Pesky would be there!) A girl at a baseball clinic! The papers had a field day.

In the afternoons my mother ran a juvenile salon. Our house was always open; people of all ages gravitated there. The conversations were adult. Our teen-aged friends came to ask questions and stayed to discuss issues—issues that were not brought up in their homes or at school: Plato and the Socratic method; the cons *and* pros of "socialized medicine" (red-flagged as a communist plot); "syphilis"—what it was and its genetic effects (*that* word was never seen in print!). My mother didn't dodge controversy; she lectured and we listened; we threw in arguments; she counter-argued and documented; and we learned to think.

In adolescence (which seemed to, and may, have lasted twenty years) I was frequently unhappy, brooding and secretive. I was not only too tall, even in high school; I was painfully thin (so stylish now!). I hated my arms—chopsticks—and for three years refused to wear short sleeves. The boys I liked didn't like me. Everyone went steady but me. Misery! My mother was right when she told me I would appeal to older and wiser men, but *then* I wanted to be popular with my peers. What good did being voted "most pleasing personality" do if it didn't guarantee a date?

Less than one year out of high school my life would change dramatically. I would meet an older and wiser man.

There were twenty-seven in my graduating class at Cape Elizabeth High School. Reluctantly I went to Smith. My high-school counselors begged me to "make good," since I was the first woman ever to be accepted from the school. How to inhibit a hick! I did badly the first term, envious of all those sophisticated preppies who jabbered in French class—in French. (Jabbering is easy if you begin in first grade.) By the second semester, I had caught on and did well enough to give Smith confidence in my high school, for many women have been accepted since. "I don't want to go four years to Smith, come back to

Maine, join the Junior League and marry a businessman!" I said. I did none of the above.

In February of my freshman year, I joined a group of Smith undergraduates who were traveling to a United World Federalist Conference at Princeton University. I believed in UWF, and had made speeches for it in high school, but I admit that the idea of meeting Princeton men was as exciting as world government.

All the Smithies were to be put up at the houses of professors. We dallied, driving through Manhattan, gawking at the skyscrapers. Dallying takes time, and we arrived at 2 AM, four hours late. A furious person greeted us—a dreadful person who swore at us! All those elderly professors sitting up, waiting. "*God damn it!*" was my introduction to John Kemeny—three little words from my husband-to-be.

John Kemeny, a fresh Ph.D. in mathematics, was the faculty adviser to the Princeton student chapter of UWF. John Kemeny, who the previous Summer had spoken all over New Jersey to every possible group asking them to call for a strengthening of the United Nations. John Kemeny, who even then was most persuasive. Who else could have gotten a chapter of the DAR to endorse enthusiastically a petition in favor of world government?

I didn't go back for my sophomore year at Smith. We were married that November, 1950.

I will be fifty at the end of 1980. I was married five years after the end of World War II (still *the* War to me). The apathetic fifties were beginning. Adjusting, understanding the ensuing social and sexual upheavals has not come easily. I was pregnant with our first child the year the word "virgin" was first used in a film and we thought, "How daring!" I am several years older than Gloria Steinem; yet I feel younger, or at least less streetwise. At 35, and approaching what was then considered middle age, I read *The Feminine Mystique* and said, "By God—Friedan's right. I haven't really thought about these things before." But the early polemics of the women's movement turned me off because I equated the movement with a diatribe against

men. Every feminist I knew was reacting to an unhappy relationship with a man. Man was the enemy, and only sisters who
agreed could be true revolutionaries or true women.

However, as the movement took hold and the rage subsided
into coherent action, I was forced to reexamine my own in-
grained attitudes and my generation's willingness not to rock
the boat. A new freedom was being offered—no, thrust upon—
women, and how would I cope with it?

In my generation, with its own set of values, limitations and
taboos, how many of us were male chauvinists because that was
the norm? How many of us listened to sexist remarks, jokes,
put-downs, and never heard them? How many of us really questioned the inequality of women? We had been conditioned by
society not to notice. An absence of women lawyers or surgeons?
I never asked, "Why not?"

I didn't question the fact that most of us (not all) at Smith
expected to, and wanted to, be married and have lots of children. A junior editorship at *Harper's Bazaar* was an interesting
interlude on the way to settling down in suburbia. Marriage
meant approval. Marriage meant security. Marriage meant legal
sex.

Sex was a lively topic of discussion at college. I remember a
rating session on our "sexual" experiences. How wicked we felt.
How innocent we were.

Of course, some of the girls had had intercourse, but they
rarely admitted it in public. It was much more exciting to discuss just how far we *had* gone—not very far at all.

A horror of pregnancy, of illegal abortion, of letting down
trusting parents, was an over-riding factor. My parents, so much
more liberal than most, never said "Don't." They never said,
"Jeannie, be a *good* girl." If they had, it would have meant,
"Be honest, be kind, be tolerant." Theirs was an implicit trust,
a trust which quenched any fires of daring or desire.

In that era homosexuality in either sex was considered a
major aberration. A retarded member of the family was kept a
guilty secret. And mental breakdowns were discussed in a tone

which implied that the person involved had little strength and no moral character.

Several girls at Smith were thrown out as possible lesbians. And after I left college the accusation that a male professor was a homosexual became a major scandal—on a *women's* college campus!

We were on our honor to report ourselves to the college's Judiciary Board if we were late signing in at night. A weekend away had to have the approval of our parents and the college. We had to state *exactly* where we would stay and with whom. I remember a statement that implied that even away from college —on vacation or in the Summer—we were representing our college and, therefore, our character must be spotless.

We knew the days when Dartmouth, Yale, Princeton and Harvard visited the campus. (Amherst didn't count; it was too near and therefore less interesting.) We were ready with our facades. Lipstick on, pageboys in place, Sen-sen ready. No boy would see us *au naturel.* Off with baggy dungarees, flapping men's shirts and loafers whose soles were held together with adhesive tape.

With envy, even jealousy, John and I discuss the freedom of choice available to the present generation—a freedom taken for granted. The easy naturalness of companionship and sex. The lack of facades. The right of a woman to want to compete with a man without being laughed at, stepped on, ignored and dismissed.

How long will this freedom last? I worry about building backlash.

John and I were from two cultures, two countries. He was a Hungarian Jew from Budapest who had reached New York in 1940—just in time. I was a northern New England WASP. Most of my ancestors arrived more than 250 years ago—Norman, English and Scots–Irish. (The public reason given for the latter's sudden departure from Argyllshire, Scotland, was religious freedom and persecution; the private story is one of sheep thieves looking for sanctuary.)

I knew few Jews. But Hitler's treatment of them must have made a great impression, for at the age of seven I wrote him a scathing letter, telling him to stop his persecution. I lived in terror for years expecting the Führer to search out my house and bomb it. I never told my parents how frightened I was and only found out when I was grown that my father had kept the letter as a souvenir!

My grandparents probably never met a Jew. I doubt they thought much about them. They did have their prejudices, however. The Ulster background with its virulent Presbyterian, anti-papist attitude seeped down through generations. A maternal great-uncle fell in love and married the upstairs maid. Just not done! But, much worse, she was Catholic. That was unforgivable. He was ostracized by his family for years. My mother insisted that he be invited to her wedding, but I'm not sure that cured the wounds.

All my grandparents were rock-ribbed Vermont Republicans (probably because the large French and Irish–Catholic population in the state were Democrats). And when many of their children and grandchildren deserted the party and became registered Democrats (not even closet ones), their reaction was: "Where have we gone wrong?"

There had never been a marriage with a gentile in John's family. Yet it was not my Yankee, Anglo-Saxon heritage that was a question. It was my cooking. John's father gave him a warning: Be prepared for bland meals! (*He* had probably eaten someone's lousy New England boiled dinner once.) John thought paprika was spicy; he was utterly unprepared for Tabasco sauce, curry powder or layers of freshly ground black pepper.

But there's precedent for the marriage. Where did Rodgers and Hammerstein look when they wanted to write *Carousel?* In Hungary. Molnar's *Liliom* was transported to the coast of Maine.

Marriage changed my life drastically. In a year and a half I went from being an immature senior at a tiny, provincial high school to being the immature wife of a professor at a world-famous university—Princeton. My friends changed. No longer my age and adolescent, they were academic giants old enough to be my parents or even grandparents. And marriage changed my status —up to a point. I wasn't old enough to drink legally, but I was married enough to chaperone Princeton club weekends. I was there to protect the morals and preach virtue to the dates of Princeton men. How much clout could I have with Smith women who had been my classmates six months earlier?

John was then in his mid-twenties, content as an assistant professor in the Philosophy Department, teaching logic and the philosophy of science. Except for one year's service in the Army, when he was drafted and sent to work as a mathematician on the Manhattan Project at Los Alamos, Princeton had been his home since he entered as a sixteen-year-old freshman.

We lived in the Harrison Street Project—a badly converted Army barracks, which included a kerosene-burning space heater that habitually became red hot, making me very friendly with the Princeton Fire Department; no doors on the closets or cupboards; a gas oven which blew up regularly; and walls so thin on both sides that we soon learned the intimate details of our neighbors' marriages—and probably they, ours. Grandly, the university announced that the barracks would be torn down within a matter of a year or so. They still stand, still housing graduate students, instructors and young professors. Oh, there has been a change. The front steps have been repainted different colors.

In 1953 John was wooed by Dartmouth and accepted an appointment as a full professor, age twenty-seven, to revitalize the College's Mathematics Department. It was a challenge for him; it was coming home for me. New Jersey could *never* hope to be New England.

I was ecstatic when I saw my new house—a duplex. "It has *doors and stairs!*" In early September, 1954, we moved in and Jennifer was born three weeks later; Robert arrived fifty-one weeks after that.

Those two children soon acted like twins and were active

enough to be quadruplets. (I have no infant furniture to hand
down. It was demolished.) There were no daytime babysitters.
There were no day-care centers. I was tied down and tired. I
ached for the time *both* would be in nursery school *at the same
time* and I could have two and a half hours of freedom! But
there, separated only by air into two age groups, the children
conversed constantly across the room. Robbie: "Jenny, come
tie my shoes!" During those hours, Jenny became the mother,
and this was not the nursery school's policy. It was considered
bad for the children. How about their mother? But the school
was adamant: One must go in the morning, the other in the
afternoon. So I prayed for kindergarten and first grade.

Later we built a contemporary house two miles from campus.
I settled into a secure, sheltered life as the wife of a tenured
professor.

But I was vaguely dissatisfied. I did all those volunteer civic
things one was supposed to do—boring. I also sang in a mad-
rigal group, took lessons in oil painting, did a couple of musicals
with The Dartmouth Players, and became heavily involved in
state politics—all fun and worthwhile part-time activities which
had a beginning and an end. I had no marketable skills; I was
trained for nothing; yet I wanted something which I couldn't
articulate.

John was becoming restless, too. In record time he had accomplished much of what he had set out to do in the Mathematics Department—building it into the finest undergraduate
teaching department in the country. He had written a dozen
books in mathematics and philosophy. He had established a
computer center—the first time-sharing system in the world,
and coauthored BASIC, a computer language used interna-
tionally. He was ready for a position in which he could decide
educational policy.

Offers began to trickle in. Then he was deluged: a deanship
of a graduate school, provostships and academic vice presidencies, and in 1969, three offers of presidencies—one from an
enormous metropolitan university.

Dartmouth's President John Dickey had announced his re-
tirement the year before, having served twenty-three years. A

search committee was formed with input from all segments of the College. Fifteen reasons why John had no chance to be picked are listed in the next chapter.

As each outside offer came in, he turned it down, secretly hoping the impossible would happen at Dartmouth. But I knew he would seriously consider and probably accept a position elsewhere soon.

I dreaded that time. I had the power to keep him at Dartmouth. He would not leave if I asked him to stay. Hanover was home, my security blanket, my nest. I wanted no change of scene, I needed the change of seasons. No desert, California or the South. And no city! But if I held him back we'd both become desperately unhappy.

The search committee interviewed other college presidents throughout the country to find out the qualities they felt were necessary in a new President. From hundreds of candidates they interviewed dozens. The search took more than a year. President Dickey was chafing at the bit.

Late in the Fall of 1969 we heard a rumor that John was on the list of finalists, but no Trustee had interviewed him!

The weekend of December 12th was decisive. On Friday, John gave a report to the Dartmouth Alumni Council on behalf of the committee on coeducation. On Saturday afternoon, he was asked by the Trustee search committee "to give them his ideas on education." That evening Dartmouth celebrated its Bicentennial with a birthday party, Charter Day, for thousands in the Field House. Walking in, I bumped into Lloyd Brace, a tall courtly man who was Chairman of the Board of Trustees. He said, "We had a very interesting discussion with your husband this afternoon."

But we knew it was too late. The Charter Day celebration was the ideal time to announce the new choice. Massive pictures of the twelve Dartmouth Presidents were hung from the ceiling. And there was a place for one other. It seemed so obvious that, at an appropriate moment during the evening, a picture of the President-elect would fill that empty space. But there was no fanfare, no announcement, no picture.

The next morning, Sunday, a colleague called John. "Have

you seen *The Sunday Times?"* In a long article, written primarily about the celebration of Charter Day, there were these paragraphs:

> Dartmouth College—the nation's ninth oldest institution of higher learning—celebrated the 200th anniversary of its founding charter here today with the distinct impression that an era was ending. . . .
>
> Soon to retire is the school's 62-year-old President, John Sloan Dickey . . . who announced . . . his intention to retire this year when a successor is chosen. The announcement is expected soon.
>
> A prime candidate, according to speculation here, is John G. Kemeny, a mathematics professor here who once worked as Albert Einstein's assistant and pioneered in developing computer time-sharing. . . .

John was sure that this "speculation" was enough to knock him out of the running. The *New York Times* reporter, talking to Alumni Councilors following John's coeducation presentation on Friday, found many of them touting his name for President. They probably hadn't even thought of him until that afternoon. But he *had* been superb. (The reporter made a lucky guess, for I know he filed that story before the search committee made its final choice!)

Two weeks later, just before Christmas, the phone rang. I answered it and shook. I knew that voice—the Chairman of the Board! Could John meet with him in Hanover after Christmas to discuss some matters of importance? We just might find the time, but how about Boston, since we had already planned a brief vacation there, and Mr. Brace lived in the area? They settled on a date and a time at the Ritz-Carlton. Superstitiously, I insisted on going down by bus. Let someone else drive.

We splurged, and for the first time had a room overlooking the Boston Common. Mr. Brace arrived, we exchanged a few polite words and then, as an excuse to leave graciously, I murmured that I had some shopping to do. Shopping! I went down to the second floor of the Ritz, the tea-room, and ordered several sherries, one after the other, whiling away the eons playing with a wooden puzzle Jenny had given me for luck and finishing the *New York Times* crossword in record time. Was I sharp! And just a bit loaded. Sherry is not called "Sneaky Pete" irresponsibly.

At last, the elevator opened, my husband bounded out, and from across the room flashed a V. He had been offered the Presidency of Dartmouth!

In the Spring of 1977 we were a foursome for dinner with Mr. and Mrs. Lloyd Brace. It was a comfortable evening—warm and open. And I confessed to Lloyd what I had really done that afternoon we met in the Ritz—I certainly didn't go shopping.

"Shopping!" he laughed. "It never occurred to me that you would!"

Now secrecy. The word must not leak until the Trustees could meet and officially confirm the choice of a new President. Secrecy meant that for one month we had to appear bemused and blank as rumors began. It also meant that I *could not* drive over to the President's House to quiz Mrs. Dickey with a million questions. Secrecy meant that Jenny and Rob had to keep their mouths shut, which they did—completely. I didn't—completely: I told the family and two friends.

The night before we were to go to Boston for that official vote, my head split into a thousand pounding pieces. Aspirin was useless. So was a furious discussion with myself that this migraine-like thing was only nerves. "John! Call the doctor! I need some codeine fast!"

John reached Josh Burnett, our family physician, briefly mentioned the headache, and that I wanted to be well by tomorrow because something very exciting was going to happen. And he told him what would happen. Doctor Burnett was a marvelous audience, excited for us and the College, and the conversation rambled on forever about the Great Event. No one remembered *me!* I was in agony. I was dying. I hissed. I moaned. I feebly waved my hand. But not until *all* the ramifications of the Presidency were gone over at least six times did

John notice my death throes. He casually mentioned that I was now writhing on the floor. And I got my codeine.

A carload went down to Boston; President Dickey drove. John was hustled off somewhere. I meekly followed Mrs. Dickey and several Trustee wives to a luncheon hosted by Mrs. Brace. What an amusing, vivacious and kind woman! Where was my stereotype of the typical trustee wife—the rigid matriarch? She didn't exist. Terror, timidity—all my fears vanished. I wasn't being accepted politely; I was gathered in and welcomed as an equal.

While I was chattering, John was in another part of Boston all alone in an anteroom waiting for the Trustee vote. Although the deliberations were only a formality, John found it strange that the Boston paper he picked up to read as he sat there had a headline above the masthead which blared: "KEMENY ELECTED DARTMOUTH'S THIRTEENTH PRESIDENT."

My Husband, the President

THE FIRST OF MARCH, 1970—Inauguration Day. A cold one, gray and damp; piles of decaying snow littered the campus. We had just reached the gymnasium where the ceremony would take place, when the sun peeped out. A good omen. But a better one was hanging from the third-floor window of a nearby dormitory. Some students had painted a bedsheet with large letters: "PRESIDENT KEMENY FOREVER."

When the committee began its search for a new President of Dartmouth, John and I jotted down numerous reasons why he would *not* be picked. It became a game. How many could we tote up?

He was a *non*-alumnus of the College.

He was born a Jew. No Jew had ever been chosen as president of an Ivy League institution.

He was a first-generation immigrant.

His accent was not British, but heavily Central European.

He attended no place of worship.

He was an outspoken liberal.

He had trouble remembering names and faces. Putting the two together was almost impossible.

He had strong opinions and voiced them frequently.

His temper could be explosive.

He was not a Republican, or even an Independent, but, God
forbid, a registered Democrat.

He was a night person and functioned badly before noon.

He was a pure mathematician and a scientist. Although he
had minored in philosophy, taught it and written a book
about it, humanists considered him a scientist only.

He was not an outdoorsman. He neither killed animals for
sport nor did physical exercise for his own health. (Although occasionally he could still play a winning game of
tennis, and he was a superb shot with a rifle.)

He smoked constantly—not a good role model for the young.

He was partially color blind, and, of course, the color he had
most trouble with was the green of Dartmouth.

What are the attributes needed by a college president? One
could list a few: He must be a superb administrator, an educational innovator and a fund-raiser extraordinaire. President
Wells, who headed the University of Indiana for almost a quarter of a century, put it more pointedly: "A president must be
endowed with the stamina of a Greek athlete, the cunning of
Machiavelli, the wisdom of Solomon, the courage of a lion—
and the stomach of a goat." But he left out the most important
quality: A president must also have the sense of humor of a
Groucho Marx.

In 1950, Wilmarth Lewis, a Yale man, wrote:

Yale's next President must be a Yale man. He must be a great
scholar—and also a social philosopher who has at his finger-
tips a solution of all world problems, ready to give the ultimate word on every subject under the sun from how to handle
the Russians to why undergraduates riot in the Spring. . . .
He must have great spiritual qualities. . . . He must not be
too far to the right, too far to the left, or a middle-of-the-
roader. . . . *He must be married to a paragon—a combination of Queen Victoria, Florence Nightingale and the Best-
Dressed Woman of the year.* (My italics!)

Try this juggling act: Keep seventeen balls in the air all at the same time while running as fast as possible on a treadmill randomly booby-trapped with potholes and boulders. Don't trip. Don't fall. And don't drop one ball. That's the Presidency.

Why is it that a full professor with a comfortable income, but a very small savings account is, on his elevation to the Presidency of Dartmouth, considered an instant millionaire by many individuals and all charitable organizations?

John makes about the same amount as an expert stone mason would *if* he worked comparable hours, but the President works for a non-profit corporation. I remember in the 1960's when he had a paid position on the Hanover School Board, another non-profit organization. Three years he served—at 11 cents an hour.

To survive, a college president must have a sense of humor. John has been endowed with an over-abundance. His humor bubbles forth—a stream of jokes. Some are bawdy or amusing or both; a few are classics. Most are dreadful!

During an office day, his staff keeps count: "That's one. That's two." If he hits three, he's ordered home.

For a one-week period I dutifully jotted down all his jokes (they filled a notebook); then after discarding, shredding and burning the bulk, I saved three for posterity:

A student we like very much wrote asking whether he could use John as a character reference. John: "Anytime you need a witness that you are a character, I am available."

We both smoke. I like lots of fresh air; he prefers stuffiness. Every night we fight about open versus closed windows. John (after losing the usual argument) grumbles: "I'm going to leave all my money to the Stale Air Fund!"

Several large pizzas and half a gallon of red wine consumed at our rural retreat. I got loaded. John: "A book, a round of pasta and you beside me in the wilderness, jugged!"

The days when a university president could endure a quarter of a century in office are gone. The job is too grueling, the pressure too intense. After a decade of coping, most find they are burned out. In the early seventies, the average tenure for a president of an American college or university was a little over four years.

On the first of August, 1977, after a tenure of seven and a half years, John became the most senior president in the Ivy League. In those seven-plus years, Harvard, Yale, Princeton, Cornell, Columbia and Pennsylvania each had a turnover; Brown had two. So now my husband is the patriarch, dignified and graying, endowed with wisdom gleaned from trying years.

Me? I just feel ancient and very creaky.

At some time during the tenure of a public figure the possibility of a portrait arises. When an alumnus offered to commission one of John, I went to New York, picked an artist and lined him up for a series of sittings. Very soon after the verbal agreement, the artist called to say that he couldn't do it, that he was dry and was giving up portraiture to meditate for an indefinite period.

A setback, but there were other artists.

John wasn't so sure. Gloomily, he recounted other rejections: "Remember, as a child in Hungary, after taking piano lessons for a year, my music teacher abruptly gave up teaching—just before my first recital? Remember, during the War, when I was an undergraduate and made the last cut on the fencing team? What did Princeton do just before my first match? It cancelled the sport for the duration!"

With great help from the Dean of Libraries, we did find another artist, a man of great talent and personality, who did not need a guru. He produced a superb portrait, and John is less morose.

When a president-elect takes office, he has usually had time to learn and absorb the intricacies of the new position. John had less than six weeks. His was on-the-job training. It was also not-quite-on-the-job training. For people *will* forget to explain that some duties begin before the oath of office.

With no idea of what was to happen to our lives, we bought tickets in November to the late Winter football banquet celebrating the Ivy championship. At Christmas, John was asked to be the next President, and was elected in January to take office in March.

This caused a commotion with the arrangements committee. What to do with a President-elect? He had bought tickets! Answer: Seat him on the dais with the other notables. (They *did not* discuss refunding us the price of the tickets!)

John sat on the dais. He relaxed—briefly. Then he thumbed through the program. He read: "Remarks by President Dickey, Speech by Coach Blackman, Major Address by President-Elect Kemeny." He ate no dinner, but he did write a major address.

Finished, he sat down to let down. Throwing out the winning game balls was the next item on the program, and, since Dartmouth was undefeated that year, there were nine. It is customary for the quarterback to do this; if he cannot, the job reverts to the President of the College. But traditions have to be flexible. The Coach announced that the quarterback had a separated shoulder. The President had bursitis, but happily there was a replacement—the President-elect. Most American boys are reared on football. John was *not* reared as an American boy. But he stood up and heroically heaved to nine player-stars scattered across a crowded room. He missed water glasses—and several players. But he did throw two spirals.

May, 1970

Two months after John took office, Nixon announced the incursion into Cambodia which was followed three days later by the murders of four students at Kent State University. None of us who lived through that week will ever be the same.

Cambodia–Kent State—a crisis. Campuses were in turmoil. Disruption, anger and a sense of fear were everywhere. Would Dartmouth erupt too? Or could a very unseasoned President make a difference?

John and I met with a group of students that weekend to explore how Dartmouth might effectively react to the Cambodia crisis. I quote from a running chronology of those days written by two student leaders, published in the *Dartmouth Alumni Magazine,* June, 1970:

> In the course of the meeting, Kemeny switched from playing the devil's advocate to exploring the possibilities of the kind of strike that was being proposed. He thought through some of the problems out loud, and suggestions as well as criticisms came from all quarters. Mrs. Kemeny was present and made a very strong argument to her husband that the community was facing a serious crisis and that there were times when even an institution such as Dartmouth had to break out of its traditional posture and respond.

Monday, following the Kent State killings, John cancelled all appointments and began a day-long series of meetings with faculty, staff and administration; he saw clusters of students representing every faction from the revolutionary SDS to the Conservative Coalition. Conflicting advice, diverse opinions flowed all day. But then the groups drifted out, and John was alone in the office with an hour to decide what to do and what to say. By chance, a live broadcast on the student-run radio station had been scheduled two weeks earlier for that evening. But events had drastically changed the topic. Using no notes, he went on the air and spoke to the entire community. I remember listening not to my husband, but to the President of Dartmouth. He spoke calmly and movingly; he urged everyone to be constructive, not destructive. I include much of that speech, for it may have been the most important one he will ever have to make:

> We are meeting tonight over the air at a time of one of the most troubled periods in American history. . . .
> I have consistently held over the years that while institutions as such cannot effectively take stands on controversial issues, individuals must take stands. . . . I am painfully aware of the fact that no college president can use this prerogative too often or he loses his effectiveness. And yet events have

taken place during the past week which make it impossible for me not to exercise this prerogative. . . .

We found a number of attacks by the federal government in Washington upon our great universities that showed, to say the least, complete misunderstanding of the feelings of the present generation of college students and a very large fraction of the college and university faculties.

And then, to all these issues, an overwhelming issue has been added. This has been the escalation of war in Indochina. . . . We find that the President is criticized by leaders of both parties . . . and yet Congress seems to be frustrated as to how it can assert its authority. This may bring about one of the most serious constitutional crises in the history of the United States. . . .

The final event, today, was the killing of two boys and two girls at Kent State University. I do not know all the details of how they died and to me the details are unimportant. . . . I can only come to one conclusion: That all of us are at fault. . . .

. . . we are faced with a call from a large number of students for the united action by the Dartmouth community to find means to express its dissatisfaction, its frustration, and to work out new methods by which a community action in unison can have an effect on the policy of this country. . . . While the word "strike" has been used, . . . this is not a strike against Dartmouth College, but an attempt . . . to unite the entire community in joint effort. . . .

I have tried to search for a precedent . . . the closest one I could find was from a minute of the Trustees of Dartmouth College. The Trustees voted, at a time of what they described as "public distresses of the present day," an early termination of the academic year. . . . It happened to be July 24, 1776.

I feel that we are now at the point of crisis. I am greatly shocked by the death of four students, which is tragic in itself and a symptom of a national malady. I am therefore taking the following actions as President of Dartmouth College:

I am suspending all regular academic activities for the remainder of this week.

Secondly, I am declaring tomorrow a day of mourning for the students at Kent State, and a day of soul-searching for the entire institution. . . .

In addition . . . I am asking faculty members to take advantage of the fact that I am cancelling classes for tomorrow to have as many meetings . . . to bring about collective wisdom as to what we can do for the remainder of this week and beyond. I am inviting the general faculty . . . to a meeting at 8 PM tomorrow in Alumni Hall. . . . I am holding it in the evening so it may be preceded by a day of soul-searching on the part of the entire faculty.

I realize that there are many who feel that regular education should not be suspended. And yet there comes a time when there are priorities over and beyond that which we have traditionally considered the fundamental purpose of the institution. I am saying that by suspending classes tomorrow we will engage in education . . . education of the deepest form where a broad community can sit down together and try to formulate its views and engage in a collective exercise of formulating plans for the future. I feel that all of us will be better educated by the end of the week as a result of this action.

With that speech he brought a divided community together.

With that speech he created a mood that set Dartmouth apart as a force for *effective* action.

With that speech he set the style of his own Presidency.

Townspeople, faculty and students conducted teach-ins and seminars, determined to make the week a learning experience unparalleled. And it was. Dartmouth medical students and undergraduates went into the towns of New Hampshire and Vermont seeking signatures on petitions of protest. They sent ten thousand signatures to Washington.

Most of the Tuck School of Business went to Manhattan. Faculty, students and the Dean spoke from the steps of the New York Stock Exchange, ridiculed and harassed by hardhats.

College undergraduates organized a lobby and went to Washington. Many members of Congress later praised the students as the most effective of any college group.

John, with faculty, administrators and students, went out on the road to talk to the alumni. Again from the 1970 article:

After a personally successful evening in Concord (N.H.), Kemeny was expansive although quite tired when the five students arrived about 11:45. Mrs. Kemeny offered brandy, coffee and cake to the five, but they elected only the coffee and cake fearing they might pass out on the Kemeny's living-room rug if they drank anything in their state of exhaustion.

On campus a special multi-paged newspaper was printed each night listing the next day's activities at Dartmouth. Dozens of volunteers typed, mimeographed, collated and delivered it to as much of the community as possible in the early morning.

Undergraduates wrote personal letters to alumni explaining what was going on and why. Confused alumni began to understand the students' side and felt closer to the campus. Long after the protest had died, letters were still being exchanged.

The *positive* action of a campus and a community did not make headlines that week. Most of the media spurned us because no building had burned, no one had died. The reactionary *Manchester Union Leader,* published by William Loeb and famous for its vitriolic editorials, did notice. (In Hanover, if one is attacked in the front page editorial, he is awarded the "Loeb-el Prize" by envious friends.) The paper attacked my husband, saying that Dartmouth "had bought another lemon." Instantly, T-shirts on campus blossomed with hand-screened lemons; students bought bushels of lemons to distribute at *Union Leader* headquarters. We asked them not to go; tempers were running high and they risked being beaten up. Several faculty presented John with a live lemon tree and a scroll stating that the lemon tree should succeed the pine as Dartmouth's symbol.

When it was over, after the days of euphoria, of incredibly hard work and exhaustion, John spoke to a rally in the Field House. Sitting on sleeping bags and blankets, three thousand students heard him say how proud he was of them; that they had accomplished much, but now they needed some sleep. When a student organizer told him: "You know, President Kemeny, you're a folk hero," John was not sure what that meant; he hoped it was a compliment. He *was* a ham—throwing lemons to a wildly enthusiastic audience. Normal classes were resumed the following Monday. Lemons autographed by the President became collectors' items.

Portrait of the President

He presides over a small university—the ninth oldest liberal arts college in the country (and older than the country) with the emphasis on undergraduate teaching, the fourth oldest medical school, the oldest graduate school of business administration and a century-old school of engineering. He has to worry about an area hotel, a ski resort, a golf course and a seventy-odd-million-dollar budget. His constituency includes 4500 students, 500 faculty, 2000 staff and administration and 40,000 very active alumni, as well as a small town whose fate has been inexorably linked to the College for more than 200 years.

He is accessible to all constituents, because that is one of the aspects of Dartmouth that makes it special. His job has been called one of the most difficult in the United States by the chairman of an enormous corporation. It can be almost impossible. And the hours spent doing it are numbing. An eighty-hour week is not unusual. He works when he is run-down, gray-faced, exhausted; he works when he is ill. He rarely calls in to cancel a day.

He still teaches two classes a year—usually one to freshmen. (He is the only president of a major institution to do so.) The courses vary from honors calculus, probability theory, computing, to an experimental course in complex systems or one in the philosophy of science. In a typical year he will lecture to faculty and students on Plato, Agatha Christie, moral problems raised by the computer and Albert Einstein.

He has refused most outside invitations. He feels he is off-campus too much already, speaking to alumni groups and fund-raising. He does sit on the boards of several foundations involved in the improvement of higher education—without pay. He does not have higher ambitions or crave more power. After the Presidency, he does not want political office; he doesn't want to head a foundation. He wants to return to full-time teaching.

He has turned down six offers in the last few years to become president of larger and richer institutions.

He loves science fiction and puzzles of any kind, and has a

secret desire to coach football. The Dodgers, whom he has supported consistently since 1941, have only one real home to him —Ebbetts Field.

He thinks Shirley MacLaine a superb woman, with Kate Jackson, Jean Simmons and Mary Tyler Moore vying for close second.

He used to have a volcanic temper, much of which came from his impatience with idiocy and the frustration of having innovative ideas and no clout. The constant stress of the Presidency has mellowed that temper and made him infinitely more patient and gentle.

He is totally honest and refreshingly frank. He never waffles and does not lie. Sometimes he is corny and quite sentimental. Always he is pragmatic and naturally moral.

He is trustworthy, loyal and irreverent.

His sense of humor is quick—sometimes too quick. His jokes are numerous and awful.

He was an early champion of the rights of minorities and women. The year before he became President, he served as the first chairman of Dartmouth's Committee on Equal Opportunity. He pushed forcefully for affirmative action. He brought coeducation to the campus. He deplores chauvinism in either sex and fights bigotry, both blatant and subtle.

He will not cut down or cut out cigarettes, he devours sinful desserts, and puts on weight with terrible ease.

He believes that too many college presidents have layers of insulating buffers between them and students. Therefore, he holds weekly office hours for undergraduates *only*—no appointment necessary. He holds live press conferences over the student radio station. The questions can be sticky, but he answers them honestly and has even been known to say, "I goofed!" The reaction to his frankness on campus is positive. The reaction of presidents at other institutions who have not left themselves open is negative. One said he is out of his mind.

He is not pompous nor pedantic. He is neither a charmer nor a gentlemanly "good old boy."

He speaks and writes the English language well and lucidly —a language he first heard at age thirteen.

He never had the luxury of the seemingly unlimited resources which poured into institutions in the fifties and sixties. He was greeted with the infamous stock market plunge of 1970. He has never had the chance to try out many of his ideas; instead much too much of his time is spent in a constant struggle against mounting costs, deficits, possible cutbacks and preventing a general watering down of the quality of education. He would be happy if he could leave office knowing he had held the College together through rough years and that its future was secure.

He recognizes only two flowers—the tulip and the rose. But at his small retreat (bought only recently out of necessity) he can sit for hours absorbing the view of birches and hemlocks and the distant Vermont mountains. He has always insisted that birds were uninteresting—until he stocked his first bird feeder. Now he's not happy until *his* nuthatches arrive.

He is a superb teacher, who revels in teaching and has the gift of making the difficult simple. He is a true genius, but he does not have neuroses, rigidity or narrowness of vision. He is an anomaly, a pure mathematician who is an outstanding administrator.

He graduated from another university. Some alumni still consider him an interloper, despite the fact that he has been on campus twenty-four years—*six times* longer than the average alumnus. He loves the College that much more.

There has to be a special relationship to something when you have lived with it through the best and worst of times for more than two decades. He believes that some change is healthy, for stagnation will decay an institution. But he does not advocate "change for change's sake." He will work as hard as anyone to preserve the true traditions of the College.

He is naturally supportive of me and thinks I am too often taken for granted. He is sensitive to my moods (which frequently oscillate) and usually keeps silent when I am too outspoken or put my foot in my mouth. He loves me very much. His loyalty is something I can absolutely depend upon. He does thoughtful and silly things to please me. (He remembers the day we met, nearly three decades ago, more often than I do.) He needs and depends on me. He, above anyone else, encouraged me to become a person. And he is proud of what I have made of my life.

He loves his children, perhaps more than they realize. And he frequently feels guilty that they are sometimes judged by others, not on their own merits, but in comparison to his.

He is neither a hypocrite nor a humble man. He knows he is a good President. He has an ego which does not need constant stroking, fawning or flattery. But once in a while, a small testimonial to a job well done helps smooth over a bad day.

Eight years after that March inauguration, a graduating senior wrote: "When I think of the best of Dartmouth, I think of you; and when I judge your greatest contribution to mankind, I judge Dartmouth. I can give no higher compliment to either the institution or the man. Thank you for the mark on my life. It is not small."

Two for the Price of One

ABIGAIL ADAMS wrote to her husband ". . . Remember the ladies. . . ." Two hundred years later we are remembered, if at all, only as an afterthought.

Take, for example, two presidential searches at private institutions:

The first search committee was small, a few trustees and faculty members. Every possible qualification of each candidate was evaluated *except* whether he had a wife. The wife's abilities, if any, were ignored. Her presence was never mentioned. She effectively did not exist. Since several of the trustees were themselves heads of very large corporations, which still evaluate potential executives' wives, this omission was odd. Perhaps they didn't realize that the wife of a university president frequently works harder and contributes more to the institution than most wives of corporate executives. Later, in documenting the search, it was agreed that future searches *must* evaluate the candidate's wife. Progress.

At the other institution, the committee was enormous. Made up of trustees, faculty, administrators, alumni and students, the diverse group bickered constantly and spent endless hours interviewing hundreds of candidates. One criterion they all agreed on was the necessity of having a *visible* president's wife. They did not spell out her role, but she was to be *involved*. The wife of one of the finalists was a practicing psychiatrist, bright and able. Her career may have knocked her husband out of the race.

In the first search all wives suffered from benign neglect. In the second, they were examined carefully. Yet both committees expected the same devotion to duty once the wife became a first lady.

The "support role" has been a tradition. Wives of public figures, wives of college presidents, have been expected to be an uncrumbling, uncomplaining column of strength. But that "support role" has expanded into one of increasing personal responsibility, and love has become a many-pillared thing.

As life has become more complex, so has the job of the university president. He has to deal with an almost infinite number of problems that didn't exist a generation ago. And each year the problems multiply.

So each year the wife's role expands. She not only has to take on her husband's personal problems and the problems of the institution, but she also is expected to be a walking encyclopedia of information about the college. If she is willing, she will be given more and more responsibility until she becomes a partner in every sense.

Dartmouth is still fairly small, but it has the complexity of a large university. And few other presidents of such complex institutions are required to preserve a tradition of accessibility. At Dartmouth there has always been a closeness between the President, his wife and their constituents.

We live on campus. Our neighbors are the fraternities. We are not protected. Our phone number is in the book. We have no gates or guards.

We must find the time to meet with faculty, students, townspeople and alumni. Meetings with members of the faculty are not left to deans or subordinates; talking to students is more important than a prestigious junket to Africa; good relations between town and gown are a two-hundred-year-old tradition. We give numerous parties to which we invite a mixed group from the College: administrators, staff, Medical School, new, tenured and retired faculty; and from the town: merchants, the Chief of Police, priests and politicians. I travel with John on College business, getting to know alumni, more than any other president's wife. At receptions we split up; he takes one side of the room, I take the other, and the same sticky questions are thrown at each of us. He trusts my answers—and my judgment.

I haven't ignored the outside community since I became the President's wife: I still work sporadically in politics, I have done the fund-raising to establish a regional community theatre, I have chaired several events for the Dartmouth arts center, I'm on the Medical School development committee and I serve as a member of an active advisory group to our large Cancer Center. But that's it.

At Dartmouth it is almost impossible to be the President's wife and have an outside career, a career with defined hours, defined vacations. My responsibilities are broad, my hours unpredictable. It was difficult enough raising adolescent children while trying to resolve all the conflicts of time and need.

Several things I would have liked to do were impossible. I couldn't be in musicals. They demanded six weeks of nightly rehearsals; I would have missed rehearsals, and the entire cast would have suffered. I couldn't be a trustee of a preparatory school: I would have missed meetings away from Hanover because of prior commitments to Dartmouth, and would have been poorly prepared because I lacked time to do homework.

The pressure to do the job without complaint is subtle but very much there. I sometimes feel caught. If I'm told: "You jumped into the job with fervor and set a style that raised expectations," I can respond that implicit expectations were *already there,* partly from the community of Hanover which knew me—what I had done in town and state affairs for sixteen years—and partly from the College constituents who *assumed* that the job would be done.

Suppose I had chosen to be less visible, taken a less exhausting role? After all those visible winters in a small community, sudden hibernation would have been difficult. And appearing only in favorable weather, avoiding difficult situations, would have caused much discussion. Disappearance during documented diseases is accepted; a cop-out from combat fatigue is not.

The commitment a president's wife gives to her job is as varied as the pattern of a crazy-quilt. A few women withdraw completely, hating the responsibility, even fearing it; others have full-time outside careers and accept no institutional demands. Some play at the job, doing as little as possible. And there are those who love what I term the "housekeeping part"—planning and hostessing—but despise public appearances. All of us are propelled like baggage on a conveyor belt, but once we reach the end, there are some of us who have tried to make the most of it, maybe even a success.

What of the presidents' wives who have full-time outside careers? I know several and the number is growing. One has a job in Washington and only appears on campus during the weekend; another is a pediatrician; a third does research and made her husband promise that her career came first, before he accepted the presidency. She does nothing as first lady— adamantly.

The choice can be difficult and raise massive conflicts. Sacrifice the career, or let the husband down?

Is it fair to ask a woman, because she is a wife, to give up a profession for which she has trained for years and devote much of her time to a quite different, many-faceted job as first lady? In the sciences, particularly, this can be disastrous. With the explosion of knowledge, a few years away from her field will make her hopelessly obsolete.

Some don't feel guilty. They can say to their husbands: "Sorry, Dear, I'm doing my thing and I'm busy." And they can say to the institution: "You didn't hire me. You hired my husband." These women may feel fulfilled and liberated, but what about their husbands?

A president's wife is under great pressure to be "liberated." There are numerous articles stressing that no wife should *have* to fill a role if she doesn't feel comfortable in it, that society shouldn't force her to, that *her* life, *her* career, *her* choice are paramount. Feminists pooh-pooh her choice, stressing the subservience of the job. They do not understand the unique nature of a college presidency. It is an all-consuming job. A partnership is needed to make it tolerable.

When an alumnus says to us, "You're a great team!," I know that a barrier has been broken. I'm not thought of merely as a quiet wife hostessing intimate little dinners or mammoth receptions. I'm seen as a representative of Dartmouth, as a person with a mind and opinions.

"Partners," "best of friends," "a team." All these phrases are true for us, but they have been overused, made trite and been bastardized by phonies.

A U.S. presidential aspirant and his wife were interviewed on TV several years ago. The couple sat cozily together on a couch, looking lovingly at each other as they answered the lead-in, mundane questions. In oozing clichés the husband spoke of their life as a "team effort." But as soon as the nitty-gritty questions began, the wife was patted fondly on the fanny and left the room (for the bedroom or the kitchen?). Politics, the main thrust of her husband's life, his all-consuming passion, was *not* included in that partnership.

Dartmouth needs two people, *full time,* at the top. Neither of us could do the job without the other. And that means having to give up some precious, private creative time to be with each other during lonesome, exciting, depressing and extremely dull occasions.

Sometimes I travel with John even when I'm not scheduled for any appearances, just to keep him company—to be someone to talk to at night.

He bolsters me when I need some ego; he only tells me to shut up when I have overgeneralized and interrupted for an hour. But then, I always question his accuracy in arithmetic.

"Behind every great man is a woman." In our case I have to say that "the man is behind the woman who is behind the man."

An impulse, symbolizing this partnership, became a tradition. At his first College Convocation John grasped my hand and together we led out the academic procession. A simple tradition, but a strong statement.

Following the inauguration of an Ivy League college president, a reception was held to honor the new president and his wife. They stood for hours, shaking hands and chatting politely to a horde of invited guests. Suddenly an alumnus strode up to the couple, slung an arm around each, and crowed to the crowd: "Two for the price of one!"

I heard that anecdote during a conversation with several Ivy League presidents' wives at Yale's Westchester County retreat. While our husbands were in conference in the room next door, immersed in their ever-continuing debate on Ivy athletics, we raised newer issues. That anecdote was true for all of us. We were frustrated at being taken for granted by much of society, doing a multiplicity of tasks for free, because we were *wives*. What about pay for a president's wife? We agreed that the idea had merit. As one woman put it, "With our expertise and know-how we could receive a damn good salary on the open market."

No matter how much I do, how much I contribute, John's paycheck is no higher. The salary that comes in is for his services only. Boards of trustees make sure that a president's compensation compares fairly to that offered at other institutions— down to the smallest fringe benefit. The one factor they ignore in that comparison is the contribution (or lack of contribution) made by the wife.

The cook, the cleaning women, the yard crew, the houseman, get paid for keeping up the President's House. I'm the supervisor of that staff, but I don't get a cent.

If my husband were single—a bachelor, divorced or a widower, he would receive the *same* salary with the *same* fringe benefits, *and* the College would have to hire a part-time hostess, fund-raiser, spokesman and housekeeper. John's reaction: "Never mind the housekeeper. I couldn't do the job without you." Is indispensability worth more than compensation?

I'm not advocating a separate salary for the President's wife.

I am advocating recognition in the President's paycheck for services well done by his wife.

Do I have more clout because I am unofficial, unpaid? Would being an employee of the College disenfranchise me, stifle me with rules? Does the fact that I am fighting for a cause (Dartmouth) or fund-raising for a five-year campaign voluntarily, without compensation, make me more credible? Does my active and public support of my husband give me greater effectiveness as a spokesman with the alumni? I don't know.

A letter from a sympathetic Trustee wife:

> . . . I have thought a lot about the bargain Dartmouth has in you, and I'm not sure anything can be done about that bargain condition. The next President's wife may be completely unable to function as you do, and how can *that* become a budget figure? The cold hard fact is that the satisfaction of being a tremendous help to John, of being enormously gifted as a hostess and enjoying a variety of interesting personalities, is going to be your only reward. Seems unfair, but very little in life is fair! . . .

What type of recognition should a working president's wife insist on as an alternative to pay? I am not an officer of the College; I am not listed in the College Directory, which lists every file clerk; I don't even have a College Identification Card— issued to *all* employees and students. I exist and perform very unofficially.

I know that to denigrate the appellation "housewife" is heresy. But I've been there for twenty years. And it wasn't particularly rewarding. I gave in and listed my occupation as "housewife," since there was no good alternative available. However, my occupation changed, and I tried to buck bureaucracy. I listed myself as "President's Wife" on my hospital card. The card was returned promptly; my occupation: housewife. John *has* succeeded on my behalf: The IRS accepts "President's Wife!"

I am thinking of an even better title bestowed on me by the editor of the *Dartmouth Alumni Magazine:* "Dartmouth's First Lady and Principal Assistant (without portfolio) to the President." That would shake up all those bureaucrats—but only momentarily.

What official recognition would I like? I would like to be made an officer of the College, but that's not crucial. I think I *should* be listed in the College Directory. What title? Maybe just "President's Wife." And I desperately want a College ID card!

For a fee, the College issues parking permits. John sent in the payment and, after a suitable delay, the stickers arrived. I was issued #1. John only got #2—but then he tries harder.

I do get unofficial recognition—a lot of it, public and private. I save my fan mail.

From two student letters: ". . . The chance to speak to the two of you personally was something I shall always remember. I often wonder how many other institutions of higher learning have presidents and presidential wives as eager as the two of you, who acquaint themselves with the students. I am certain that you have heard all this before, but Dartmouth is lucky to have the two of you around. . . ." And from another: "You're such a refreshing person! Thank God for wonderful, 'normal' people like you! And imagine that—a *President's* wife! . . ." From an alumnus: ". . . So many Dartmouth people feel that they own a piece of you both, I often wonder how you maintain your peace of mind. . . ." And in public, from the Chairman of the Board of Trustees, David McLaughlin, at several huge Dartmouth dinners around the country: ". . . I'd like to stop here just for a moment to introduce the first lady of Dartmouth, a person to whom the Trustees—and I think all of us—owe a deep debt of gratitude."

And from my husband: In front of six hundred people he said ". . . You don't know how many times she has made me look good. . . ." Publicly *and* privately he is my greatest advocate.

But there are stirrings, even rumblings, among my generation of presidents' wives. What will be the attitude of the next generation? When the wife of the president of a small, outstanding, non-Ivy League college recently told her Board of Trustees, "I like my job. I do it well. But you must know we are a vanishing breed." She may well have been foretelling the future.

Recently, I polled a group of young women, students and young administrators, after an evening-long give-and-take discussion on my views and my responsibilities. "How many of you, now knowing the expectations and numerous responsibilities, would accept being a president's wife *without* some form of official recognition? How many here would give up a career, when at most institutions the presidency has become a two-person job?" *Not one* young woman answered unequivocally in the affirmative.

A month later I read a piece in the Dartmouth alumnae newsletter. I quote from a woman graduate of the class of 1976 who found herself, at first unwillingly, helping her husband politically: "And now for an unexpected and serious conclusion, I must confess that a formerly liberated and skeptical Dartmouth coed can find happiness and fulfillment through marriage. At least in my case, it certainly gives direction and purpose to both career and leisure activities. The previous sentence was a paid, political advertisement for ———" (her husband).

No woman that evening at my house knew her future. And no one knew whether or not she had fallen in love with a yet-to-be public figure or college president. Love is really the bottom line.

Home Is Where the Hearth Is

WE HAVE *seven* hearths with fireplaces, which draw when we remember to open the dampers. But the House is *not* a home.

It is on loan for the duration. Almost everything inside belongs to the College. All we contribute is wear and tear.

I questioned the decision to build the President's House on fraternity row. It is smack in the center of student activity, and the exuberant noise can be unbearably high. Our accessibility is also high.

I researched and found that the planners had not been idiots. In the twenties the campus was smaller. There were no dormitories on the back side, most of the street was faculty–town residential. Only later did the fraternities buy up the existing houses or build new ones. The neighborhood deteriorated rapidly!

The Board of Trustees suggested that they might build a new house, since the President's House was so enormous. But we both felt that renovation was all that was needed. It seemed important then—and still does—for the President and his family to live on campus.

How often does one have the chance to redecorate a twenty-five-room house completely, have someone else pay the bills (much larger than estimated) and then live in it?

In a brief period, with no experience, I had to redo this immense house. I did have unstated *carte blanche* from the Board, which I used to a maximum—mine, I think, not theirs.

What exquisite timing! We started in late winter ordering lamps, furniture, carpeting and curtains. Then the remodeling, painting and papering began. For weeks my dreams were nightmares of suffocation as I was caught in a vortex of swirling swatches of color. Three months later the stock market plunged. I am told the College lost eight million in one day on paper, and the financial crunch was on. But not for me! No curtailing for the duration, for all the orders were in—just! I got the house I wanted. Visitors like it, alumni are proud of it and the ambience is often conducive to large donations. (Someday I'll tot up how much money has been raised after a good meal.)

Beginning in late March, 1970, we began shopping for furniture at New York wholesalers. I wanted as much of an oriental feeling as possible. We ordered a large ivory rug from Hong Kong with designs in shades of apricot, and then worried that the cable would be garbled and so would the colors. But seven months later, on a slow but sure boat from China, a flawless rug arrived.

I raided the antique collections left to the College. Six of Daniel Webster's dining-room chairs were donated by Strawbery Banke. I appropriated an entire set of antique bedroom furniture from Dartmouth's retreat on Squam Lake.

Pawing through the College's art collection was a decorator's dream. Buried deep in basement vaults or in dusty attics were paintings, prints, pots and porcelain. Stored, they could not be seen; but in the President's House, they could.

I chose a small, unobtrusive Chinese painting on silk. Perfect for the best guest bathroom. But after seeing the valuation, I changed my mind. Not even I will hang $5000 over the toilet!

I did take a Chinese tombstone and a Nepalese brass canister (for yak milk?) from the College Museum. The curators offered, pleaded with me to take a stuffed mammal—anything from mouse to moose. How about a four-foot replica of the *Nina*, a six-foot Chinese cloisonné vase or a cape of shimmering peacock feathers in mint condition? I declined. What does one do about an infestation of moths in a peacock cape?

I mixed in a few of my own pieces—a Thai buddha, a rose-

wood Chinese carving, a black lacquer box, a late nineteenth-
century painting of New Hampshire done by an itinerant artist,
hunks of quartz and amethyst, shards of Roman glass picked up
in my own private dig in Israel, a piece of modern sculpture
done by a Dartmouth sophomore.

The kitchen, dismal and dark, a monument to golden oak,
depressed me. There was even a dumb-waiter. Pull out, tear
down. I was ruthless. But demolition is expensive. Why does it
cost as much to destruct as to construct?

When the new cabinets were ready, the head of the College
paint shop and I tried fourteen variations on a theme of dark
chartreuse. He may have called it by another name after two
days of my having to see each shade in bright light, little light,
wet, partially dry and very dry before I shouted, "Stop! That's
it!" About the color of good pea soup, it contrasts well with the
teal-blue, light yellow and white of the kitchen. Bright chartreuse shrieks; dull chartreuse whispers of several unmention-
ables.

As a reminder of the good old days, we left the call-board in
the kitchen. It is connected to mother-of-pearl buttons in almost every room. We left the room buttons, too. Guests may
push them as often as they wish; just nothing will happen.

The most popular attraction in the House is the set of needlepoint seats for twelve Chippendale dining chairs done by Mrs.
Dickey. Each chair symbolically represents the accomplishments
of one of the twelve previous Presidents of Dartmouth. After
every tour of the House, someone asks when will I *do* my husband, number 13? I have a stock answer: "Who seats thirteen
for dinner?" I've never done needlepoint. I plan to leave the
entire problem to spouse number 14!

The living room is the loveliest room. Even a European
Rothschild commented on its beauty. Gold and apricot, celadon
and ivory. Japanese prints, a Coromandel screen, Thai lacquer
boxes and Healy's portrait of Mrs. Daniel Webster looking very
sweet, but slightly pained. (Perhaps because she was the *second*
Mrs. Webster and had to endure Daniel's old age and special
infirmities.) I did ask the College carpenters to make a set of

doors to the living room—ones that would *shut out* dogs, cats and teenagers.

The House was a gift to the College from Mr. Edward Tuck in the middle twenties when money was flowing—particularly from Mr. Tuck, who not only was extraordinarily generous to Dartmouth, but who also made his donations with no strings attached.

How many rooms in the House? What counts as a room? Is an area in the basement 10′ by 10′ containing an old freezer, sink, cupboards, flower pots and assorted junk a large closet or a small room? I'll settle on twenty-five.

I know we have four floors; ten bathrooms (five with tubs— the wonderful long and wide hotel kind); seven fireplaces (and hearths); six staircases; eighty-plus doors (each with two brass knobs which are polished when we remember); twenty-odd closets; innumerable built-in cupboards and cabinets; ten chandeliers; over three hundred feet of bookshelf space (filled); a separate three-car garage; and a walk-in safe.

The safe caused me some embarrassment. It contained all the House silver, and one warm Spring evening before we moved in, I had an irresistible urge to count it. I worked the combination in just under fifteen minutes by the light of a 25-watt bulb. What sport pulling out tons of carefully wrapped flatware and serving pieces. I was now endowed with desperately needed oyster forks, fish knives, berry spoons and enough urns or some-such to contain the ashes of the entire alumni body. I was surrounded, covered, almost crushed to death by a fortune in silver (much of it plated, I later learned). And in that position I was caught (in my own House) by two campus policemen on the prowl.

On the first floor alone there are over three hundred separate panes of glass to be cleaned periodically. I'm not too fussy about the windows; if the view is only blurry, I ignore them. Complete obscurity does, however, move me.

Much of the basement was built for a more leisurely time. A summer kitchen connects to a 40′ by 40′ meeting room, which we use only for student groups, and off this are two elegant bathrooms. I'd like to move just one of those bathrooms to the first floor. It is desperately needed to replace the minute lavatory which hides off the coat closet.

An entire wing on the second floor—four bedrooms, two baths—housed the live-in staff, which was on hand at all times. Our staff comes in daily, but they don't live in. Our choice.

The Cast of Characters

The staff at the President's House is an extension of my family. They can be stubborn and very loyal. When I become exasperated, so do they. I sometimes yell and most of them yell right back. I'm training the shyer ones.

All five are natives of New Hampshire or Vermont. Several commute nearly fifty miles a day.

I worry about their families and their ability to subsist on their pay; I work hard to raise it. I write letters on their behalf, and have been known to chew out an entire administrative office over "the rules"—a mountainous maze of bureaucratic red tape and idiocy.

I know they worry about me. When a call came from the hospital that the cancer I had contracted hadn't spread, several of the staff burst into tears of relief.

Delia Perkins has been with me since 1966; the others I inherited in 1970, and we had to get used to each other. I do things differently or don't do them at all.

They have become accustomed to my impulses; they put up with my sloppiness; and they are resigned to my large family of cats—all shedding in the wrong places in the wrong season.

I dislike uniforms for daytime, and I suggested slacks for the women in winter. Warmth is more important than formality.

Reg Allen had to get used to cooking strange dishes with non-New England names like *"lecso," "körözött,"* and *"pörkölt."* She will never be able to read my handwriting.

Doug McBain has had to endure my sending him downtown

constantly to pick up odd items I forgot. He is also getting used to my correcting him on gardening techniques, about which I know nothing.

Carol Johnson has learned that, if she hides the boxes of junk which I *am* going to sort someday, I won't miss them for a year, and we can have a clear pathway to the bureau and the bed.

Viola Gilson knows how to serve sixteen people in the plant room, adroitly skirting the plants. She is also adept at giving a capsule history of the House to hundreds of visitors.

When a helper is ill, there's another to do double duty—even I. At one luncheon, I waited on twenty guests. The Trustees were so overcome that several stood up to help me. They were rather good waiters. I may hire them periodically.

On paper, each staff person is listed as having one job. This is nonsense.

Doug is the "houseman," but he is the "everyman" and the only full-time employee. (The others work two days a week.) He even waits on table now and chauffeurs us to cities and planes. He knows that as soon as I say: "It's only snow flurries, Doug," we'll hit a blizzard and drag into Manhattan ten hours later.

Reg is the "cook," but she cleans silver and dirty stoves, mends seams and arranges flowers better than I.

Carol and Delia are listed as "cleaning women," but they, like Doug, do anything and everything when necessary. Carol waits on table; Delia passes hors d'oeuvres. They do the laundry and a hundred other odds and ends.

Viola does most of the ironing and serves at dinner parties. She will come in at a moment's notice to help out. And her husband, Maurice, *not* on the College payroll, vacuums to perfection!

They meet interesting people who take time to talk to them —Walter Cronkite, Mary Tyler Moore. Captain Kangaroo carefully wrote down twenty names of the staff's children, nieces, nephews and grandchildren and then remembered each one with a personalized autographed picture.

Their ages range from thirty-five to seventy-five. We listen to each other's fury and fears, political views, gripes and gossip.

We started together. I hope we will end together, for I could not handle my job without them.

What have been the House's problems? Heating, for one. There are two thermostats controlling the entire House. And both are on the first floor. The temperatures on the four floors range from dry desert heat and tropical mugginess to Arctic cold or drafty dampness. The thermostat can be set for 65, but the thermometer may register 80. We are on the College's heating system and, since the oil crisis, are monitored with every other building and rated for conservation. Anyone can check the books and find that in 1973–74 our performance was embarrassingly low. But then we weren't eligible for the weekly award that went to those dormitories with a good record—a keg of beer.

The buzzer under the dining-room table had to go. No matter how often College electricians rewired it, the damn thing gave off a jolting charge. I've switched to another age and ring my great-grandmother's brass bell instead.

Then, of course, there is the noise. We are buffeted by boisterous activity. The solution was serendipitous: After suffering for two Summers from heat waves that belong in Houston, we invested in a few window air-conditioners and discovered an extra feature: The fan and its gentle hum broke up sound waves. Fraternity newsletters delivered to residents within hearing distance announced an impending outdoor rock concert with this advice: ". . . for those who may find the noise level unbearable, it might be wise to jet to Paris, or try a fan, highly recommended by Mrs. Kemeny."

Then there were the bats. When the carpenters and the cabinet makers left, the paperhangers and painters arrived. By then it was warm enough to paint; so off went the screens, up went the windows and in came the bats. For at least a year Rob and I became expert bat-catchers, ferreting them out from their favorite hiding places in the top braces of venetian blinds. Our weapons? A wastebasket with cover, a tennis racket and a lot of courage.

I made a few mistakes. On the walls of the front hall is a

muted gold-washed paper with scattered panels of bamboo and oriental birds. "Gold-washed" does *not* mean washable. Every touch means a muddy-ochre fingerprint. Hand prints are larger and muddier. There are hundreds of these on the wall leading up to the second floor. It appears that the banister on the staircase is ignored.

The children wallowed in long hot showers, sloshing the water all over the bathroom. The water had to go somewhere— down through the ceiling into the main hall. Great bubbles appeared in the plaster and dribbled on guests. The plasterer visited semi-annually.

Cats' claws gravitate to grass cloth. It shreds so nicely. Dogs confuse soft wool rugs with Spring grass. They stain so nicely.

Finally, I convinced myself that Dartmouth was informal and the House should look lived in. And if one looks closely, it is *very* lived in.

The House was placed so that the southern entrance on Tuck Drive framed Vermont's Mt. Ascutney twenty miles down the Connecticut River. A spectacular mountain—over three thousand feet high—a gentle Matterhorn, gentian blue in Summer, flinty blue in Winter with ski trails lightly chalked. The view is no more. A dormitory obscures it.

The grounds—about four acres—are lovingly cared for by a crew from Buildings and Grounds. From the first warm day in Spring to the end of Indian Summer, the sloping lawns on the southern side become a beach resort for clusters of sunbathing students. And several grassy areas are now well-worn paths made by thousands of undergraduates taking short-cuts.

Each Spring the crew arrives to fertilize, roll, water and revitalize the lawns. But if this doesn't work, there *is* an alternative. A visit to the sunken garden where we would give our first outdoor reception was traumatic. "Does it always look like this?" I groaned, as I surveyed a desert-scape of burned, dead scrub. "Nope" was the reassuring answer. Three days later the reception was held on a lawn as verdant and lush as those five-hundred-year-old masterpieces at Cambridge University. A miracle? Nope. A sod farm.

The front yard: That lawn will bear our mark for years. It's immense and flat, a marvelous place to play games—gentle games like croquet. But Rob and some high-school friends appropriated it for touch football. The terrible damage they did was dug up and the worst areas resodded. The lawn lives again —jagged mosaics of incompatible greens.

Magnificent trees, hardy northern types, form backdrops, glades. Clumps of white birch, tough old maples, beech, a butternut, shad and those few remaining elms which have not yet succumbed to Dutch elm disease.

The clump of white birch I look at today is not the same clump I saw yesterday. When the bronze birch-borer burrows, the clump is replaced immediately with a healthy one of exactly the same size.

For privacy, Mrs. Dickey had a break of hemlocks planted in the back and two yews in the front. The yews make it possible to sit in the library and not be stared at from the street; the hemlocks make it possible to sunbathe on the stone patio out of view of the dorms beyond. At times the flagstones are blistering hot, so I move my chair to the other side of the trees on *my* lawn. The day I glimpsed a young man watching me from behind what he thought was the safety of his dorm window, I didn't flee. Instead, I waved pointedly at him. Caught, he abruptly disappeared, pulling his curtain to blush in private, I presume. I've seen no peepers since.

One tree had to go: a sycamore. Its exact age was unknown, but estimates ranged upwards from a century. It was a favorite of Robert Frost. During the forties and fifties, as a guest at the President's House, he always chose the same bedroom—one with the best view of the tree. I heard him read his poems once; I never met him. But I like to impress guests: "Would you like the Robert Frost bedroom?"

President Dickey warned us that in its old age that sycamore had a habit of dropping branches indiscriminately. The College spent much money feeding and babying the tree, but the Spring when it barely leaved was a signal, its death-knell. And it seemed reluctant to go—tough, hard wood that made a saw bounce.

One real hazard still exists. The House has a steep roof of slate shingles. After thaws, tons of snow will let loose over the front door. All guests are warned of the impending avalanche.

Near the back steps is a basketball hoop put up for a teenaged son, now grown and away. It is a magnet for small groups of students. For years now, from Spring to Fall, from noon to dusk, the thump, thump, thump of the ball is constant. If I remove it, I could be accused of tearing down a tradition.

Old-fashioned lilacs, Japanese euonymus and rhododendrons flower. So do hydrangeas, which I hate, except dried.

The sunken garden, one side a bank of ground cover and flowers, dotted with ferns as tall as small palm trees and Japanese lanterns hanging from evergreens, resembles a tropical garden on a velvet Summer's night—unless it's freezing, which is also quite possible on a Summer night.

The flower and vegetable garden is the envy of the neighborhood, as is the enormous compost heap. Many of the perennials have been there for years—peonies, lupine, lemon lilies. Tuberous begonias ordered every year from southern California thrive in the northern Summer. We personally paid for several pairs of fruit trees—hardy peach and pear, which probably won't bear until the year after John leaves the Presidency. But we do have raspberries—eighty-four quarts last year.

Sweet corn, freshly picked, is a passion. But I've got to stop growing zucchini. Tiny, I like them. But zucchini are clever at hiding, at being missed, until they are ready to burst out—monsters.

Each year we lose half our flowers and vegetables to marauding moles and mice, dogs, deer, raccoons and birds. What the woodchucks don't get the squirrels do. Last year my Hav-a-Hart trap caught seventeen squirrels and two skunks. But what does one do with a skunk that wanders out of his prison and then wanders right back in again?

We built our first house, a beautifully designed glass and cedar contemporary, a bit outside of Hanover. At our housewarming, Christina Dickey, who had lived for fifteen years in the large,

Georgian President's House said: "Jean, I want a house just like this!" Eleven years later she had one, a beautifully designed glass and cedar contemporary, a bit outside of Hanover, and we are now living in that large Georgian house!

Someday we'll move to a much smaller house. There will be a minimum of landscaping and no grounds crew to cultivate and cut the grass. There won't be grass; pine needles are less work. Our only raspberries will be the encroaching kind, to be pulled out ruthlessly. There won't be receptions in a mammoth sunken garden. I won't have receptions; I won't even have a tiny sunken garden. I do plan to have a few hardy flowers which will probably bloom more profusely if I ignore them. And I will entice wild animals, not trap them. If porcupines like petunias, let them have a feast.

Protocol
(or the Lack Thereof)

I was the President's wife for about a month when I asked a well-known and accomplished hostess, "How do you know what to do?" (At that time I thought the only job of a president's wife was entertaining.) She replied, "Try to remember what your mother did."

At first that seemed like a sensible suggestion. My mother never had to entertain forty people at the same time, but she did give dinner parties. The trouble is I don't remember how she gave the dinner parties. And suppose my mother had *not* been a genteel New Englander, but the daughter of a coal miner in Appalachia or a tenant farmer in Mississippi—what would I remember about how she did it?

Protocol is defined by Webster as: "A rigid, long established code prescribing complete deference to superior rank and strict adherence to due order of precedence and precisely correct procedure (as in . . . ceremonies and military service)."

My first encounter with protocol occurred when I was ten. It was exciting news that a new heavy cruiser would be named for the capital of Vermont. According to protocol, the citizens of the capital were expected to present a silver service for the officers' use. The citizens of Montpelier wanted to buy an extra gun for the cruiser instead. My mother, delighted with the Vermonters' common sense, teased a friend, a captain in the Navy. He was outraged. "A cruiser *must* have a silver service.

It is a tradition!" Our old friend saw combat in the South Pacific; I often picture him on the deck of his ship, all guns out of action, vainly trying to pelt the Kamikaze with silver coffee pots.

I'll never become used to protocol. It's silly, outdated and elitist. It's rigid and stifling.

I have never really worried where the dessert spoon is placed —to the right of the plate or above it; nor do I care about the position of the wine glass in relation to the water goblet; if the point of the pie is not at six o'clock, I do not fret; nor do I notice that the patterns on the dinner plates are not set symmetrically. Why should I? Who cares if the china doesn't always match, if the water goblets are of different sizes and shapes, that we never have enough soup spoons and some guests must sip from teaspoons or berry spoons? How many people have been shocked that at times Viola must serve from the right? It's either that or a collision with the Christmas cactus.

"Precedence" and "precisely correct procedure" are code-words for a kind of formality that is unnatural and uncomfortable, at least for me. I didn't come to the job and decide to be different. I didn't begin by defining my style. That style—very loose, easy, warm and somewhat haphazard—evolved and finally became my trademark. I managed to raise the children without reading a book on child-rearing. Yes, they drove me bats at times, but I didn't turn to Chapter X to find out why. Why then should I rely on Post or Vanderbilt as the ultimate authorities? I'll manage again, doing it my way.

I abhor the idea that I must treat people differently; that superior rank and deference go together; that seating arrangements are strictly prescribed; that employees of the College be split into two Christmas parties—faculty and officers *vs.* staff— or that every whim of a famous person must be granted, no matter how much anguish it might cause the hosts or other guests. At a very small dinner (eight or so) I do put the eldest guest of honor on my right. But at most large dinner parties my seating arrangements are casual—first come, first sit. I have used place-cards (simple ones with the Dartmouth seal), but only three times in more than nine years. I have a single College Christmas party—all employees are equal. I will not kowtow to rank, class or whims.

Perhaps at times I try too hard to break down rigidity; I have had some sensitive souls protest that they were not seated near enough a guest of honor, and a faculty wife once complained that the faculty should not have to mix with plebians at the Christmas party!

I have done my best to kill protocol at Dartmouth. The act strikes me as justifiable murder.

Maybe it all started when, as a new faculty wife, I was invited to my first tea at the President's House in Princeton. I was twenty. Dressed in my one good wool dress, gloves, sensible pumps and a chaste hat with veil (we wore veils then), I was nervous before I rang the bell. Things went downhill from there. The house was exquisite; the furnishings pristine. Had anyone ever touched, sat on or walked upon them? The President's wife? I must have met her, though I have no recollection of doing so. I am sure she was a kind lady, but I only remember feeling like a humble subject in the presence of a queen. The other faculty wives who chatted easily with one another seemed so mature, so much older and more sophisticated than I—and they were. I didn't know anyone, nobody introduced me to the others and I didn't have the gumption then to introduce myself.

The china was paper-thin; the silver (which must have been in the family for generations) seemed as new and unscratched as a wedding present. (Probably it was buffed lovingly every day.) I had visions of slopping my tea on the oriental or fragmenting the priceless cup and saucer on the polished floor. My hands had palsy. Even worse, the tiny sandwich perched on the edge of the saucer might slip as I took a step. Squashed sandwich.

Those sandwiches! They are called finger sandwiches. These, however, were fashioned after the digits of an infant—and I was hungry! Coffee for breakfast, and no lunch in anticipation of tea in the British tradition. There were no trays scattered in easily accessible places; the waiters passed them silently, for-mally—and only occasionally. At those rare times when a tray swept by me, I was tempted to grab a handful of sandwiches and gulp them down. But that would have been unseemly. The other alternative would have been to stalk the waiter, shadow-ing and snitching, but I lacked the expertise.

I returned home starving, thoroughly cowed by the stiffness, the formality, the lack of warmth and the pretense of being made to feel welcome.

And I wailed to my husband, "This is the first and the last! Don't *ever* ask me to go to another!"

Understanding and sympathetic, he soothed me. *"Honey, I promise you'll never have to set foot in a President's House again!"*

Ever since I had luncheon at the University of Pennsylvania's Museum of Art, I've changed my ideas on centerpieces. I had rather hoped to take the table's centerpiece home, but Mrs. Meyerson said, "No." It was only a small one—an Egyptian God. But I did steal the idea. I rarely use flowers now; in their place I've substituted green jade birds or a single large quartz crystal. For buffets with a theme: France, a large color photo-graph of a chateau, garlic buds, a hunk of cheese, and a copper crepe pan; Hungary, a carved and decorated box, a tulip and a can of Hungarian paprika; for the Middle East, a Greek head, Cypriot pots and a 2000-year-old Persian dagger. New England is easy: rainbow-colored pieces of sea-washed glass, mussel shells, and my grandfather's nickel pocket-watch from Waltham.

In some circles, it still seems terribly important socially for formal coffees and teas to be given—but not in my House. They have always bored me and I never saw the advantage of being asked to "pour." It is an over-rated position. My spigot always malfunctioned; either it let out only a few dribbles, or gushed, flooding the tablecloth.

I have no Autumn affair at Dartmouth for new faculty wives —or spouses. I have no party for new faculty couples. I avoid confining the function to just one inbred group, a teaching department or professional school. They see each other every day. Why not broaden their outlook? So I mix people at a cocktail party—but not a tea.

I have had trouble with the Dartmouth Wives' Association, because there *are* student husbands also. I once suggested that the organization change its name to fit the times (e.g., The Dartmouth Spice Association). They haven't yet, and no males have come. But hopefully they will when the name has been changed, and they learn that I offer little formality, no tea cups to balance and whiskey sours.

What makes entertaining an art? Why does an evening zing or fall flat? Why does a dinner party served in a Louis Quinze dining room on Crown Derby seem interminable? Or a meal impeccably cooked à la française immemorable?

A couple of boors at the table can overpower a delicate sauce. Nothing spoils a party more than an unenthusiastic hostess. The lack of enthusiasm is all pervading. As she recounts the awful day spent preparing the dinner—the disasters, the tiredness, the long hours—each bite tastes worse.

Stimulating conversation will conceal the variety of china and the good but inexpensive meal. I have started an evening quite sure I won't be able to finish and find I am drawing energy from my guests. As they are leaving, I am really sparkling.

Forty people will come for a pre-football-game luncheon. I will have only one hour and a quarter to give Trustees, administrators, faculty and their spouses cocktails, feed them and then get them on the bus in time for the kickoff. Protocol here is impossible.

The luncheon marks the end of a grueling two- or three-day Trustees' meeting. Everyone's exhausted and wants to let down and drink leisurely. And I want them to—but I also have to get them fed.

I have devised a football luncheon menu which consists of a varied and interesting cold plate and a non-meltable dessert which can be set out ahead of time. Those who want one cock-tail have time to sit down, chew and digest; those who want three cocktails will have to gulp their lunch before I clang the bell (and sometimes yell) to announce the imminent departure of the bus.

Some day a course should be offered for all public figures en-titled, "How to shake a thousand and one hands a night." (Sub-titled "And preserve those hands for another day.") A receiving line can be a painful experience, a test of fortitude. Herewith a few tips from an "old hand":

1. *Do not wear rings.* Rings become lethal weapons when ground into your fingers. That slippery feeling may be blood—not perspiration.

2. *Avoid Winter receptions.* (Unfortunately, we hold an annual Christmas party for 2500.) A reception line held in the dead of winter deteriorates into a contest of which guest has the iciest hands. Touching my cheek is a good test: The more I cringe, the colder the hand.

3. *Beware the hearty gripper.* He invariably has the longest line of chatter and will crush your fingers more unmercifully with each punctuation mark. Don't be a martyr; grimacing only en-courages him. Step on his toe.

4. *Use both hands.* This action is called "the grand right and left" and resembles that movement in a square dance when one is propelled rapidly forward. As the guest is swept by, you can smile sadly at the brief time you had together.

5. *Never, never reshake a hand.* Some guests feel obligated as a matter of politeness to reshake your hand on leaving. There is nothing in the rules which allows him two shakes for the price of one.

After all these precautions, do not despair when you examine your hands the morning after. Most of the splotches *will* disap-pear in two or three days.

"Never entertain a President!" was a maxim left to me by Christina Dickey.

She did. In the early fifties President Dwight D. Eisenhower arrived at Dartmouth to give the Commencement address. He took over the entire second floor for his stay at the President's House. The President slept in the Dickeys' bedroom, and the Dickeys moved to the third floor.

The Secret Service evacuated all dormitories and fraternities in the vicinity of the President's House. They were everywhere, including the bushes surrounding the House, where the Dickey children took great delight in ferreting them out and crying, "Boo!" The Secret Service was not amused.

Since the President had most of his meals on campus, Mrs. Dickey's only responsibility was a breakfast. But that breakfast! She searched for exotic fruit and melons; she loaded the refrigerator with chops, kippers and country sausage; she had thick fresh bread, jams and marmalade ready, and, just in case, ham and hollandaise sauce for eggs benedict.

Morning: "Mr. President, we can offer you almost anything. What would you like for breakfast?"

"Grapefruit and black coffee."

When Mrs. Dickey advised me, "Never entertain a President," she meant "of the United States."

A possibility arises that we may do so for the President of Venezuela. He has accepted in principle the idea of giving a guest lecture at Dartmouth in conjunction with a state visit to Washington.

I worry. Horror stories of repression are pouring out of Latin America. Will the students protest? I ask an authority on that area. "There'll be no demonstrations. He has the freest, most open government in South America."

Now John is worried. For I have announced that since Venezuela is one of the members of OPEC, that since *all* of Dartmouth's heating fuel comes from Venezuela and is *very* expensive (in fact has added 1 million dollars annually to the College's budget since 1973), I shall not very subtly remind the President of that fact. I'll scatter empty gallon jugs around the House and then give him a special guided tour of the rooms. He can hardly miss the labels: "#6 Crude. Please fill me."

John is relieved: He will not have to try to restrain his wife. The President is having long conversations with Carter and cannot make it.

He may come yet. I'm saving my jugs.

The wife of the United States Ambassador to the Soviet Union wrote a letter to a national magazine. She objected strenuously to the magazine's report that a party at the Embassy was "hosted" by the Ambassador, remarking satirically that it was *she,* not the Ambassador, who had planned and organized the party. Not that she was taking anything away from the Ambassador's role, but she did feel that wives in these positions should get some credit.

Occasionally this can still happen at Dartmouth. Invitations may still read: "Come and meet the President in his garden." (It's my garden too; I am there greeting guests, *and* I have planned that reception.) But usually notices sent out by an office at Dartmouth or the alumni clubs will say: "Reception hosted by John and Jean Kemeny" or "Come to a banquet and meet John and Jean Kemeny." I did not initiate this change; my husband did.

Wives are now invited to most alumni functions. They also sit next to their husbands at the head table on the dais—not at tables specifically reserved for wives as they once did.

We may have gently trained Dartmouth and its alumni to give women credit and to give up male chauvinism, but we have not reached *The Boston Globe*—a paper usually known for its fair and liberal policies.

I quote from that paper, Sunday, May 8, 1977:

Friday, February 17, 11:00 PM, Dartmouth College President, John Kemeny, is the host of a reception in his elegant home on Fraternity Row. Mingling in a setting of oriental rugs, antiques and American primitive paintings are College trustees, faculty and administration, and important visitors from the worlds of politics and finance. They have gathered to meet the guests of honor, a group of distinguished Dartmouth alumni returning home, but these particular alumni are not scholars or businessmen, or even a victorious football team. They are collectively, *Pilobolus,* the modern dance company born and bred at Dartmouth during the early 1970's, a group which has achieved fame and occasional notoriety with its original combination of athletics and dance. . . .

There *was* a reception at our House; *I* planned it; *I* helped cook for it; *I* was visible greeting guests, conversing, circulating, checking that there was enough liquor, enough food. And *I* decorated the damned House!

The reporter who wrote the article was one of the guests at our reception, spoke to me, saw me working and then blithely brushed the female half aside. The reporter may be an expert on the dance, but she is an MCP.

When serving guests, it is wise to learn what *not* to mention. Do not confess the disasters that occur in the kitchen. What your guests don't know won't usually hurt them.

In Budapest, John's mother entertained frequently. It was still a time of ice-boxes, ice-men and huge blocks of ice. One of her specialties was a rich mousse sculptured into the shape of a bird or animal. The shape would hold *if* the ice-box was cold enough. And to the oohs and aahs of guests, the masterpiece would be triumphantly borne in for dessert. If, however, the temperature was wrong, the shape would settle into an unrecognizable mutant. Ingeniously, John's mother would transfer the mousse into individual parfait glasses, and no one was the wiser —until John's father invariably commented: "Oh, I see the sculpture melted again!"

The hazard here was the husband; I do not have the same problem, for *I* am the one who usually confesses. I have learned after many slips to *keep my mouth shut.* Here are a few very important *don'ts:*

Do not point out that the casserole sitting on the table was not originally cooked in that dish, but transferred abruptly—

and that the inch of burned matter in the bottom of the original dish is now soaking in hot soapy water.

Do not mention that a sauce has curdled; make them believe it always looks like cottage cheese.

Do not panic if the cork on your French Bordeaux crumbles and the first sip is just-palatable vinegar. Conceal the bottle with a napkin and point out how chic it is to drink the really robust peasant wine of the Italian countryside. (Then go and swear at your storekeeper who insists on storing his cases of wine straight up!)

If you are making hot hors d'oeuvres and the cookie sheet slides out of the oven before you expect it to, don't tell the guest that you scraped the filling off the kitchen floor and re-applied it. There really isn't much difference in flavor.

If your guests are rabid supporters of worthy causes and comment favorably on the wine—the smoothness and bouquet of the Burgundy, en carafe—the better part of valor, or cowardice, is not to mention it's "Gallo Hearty." (After all, you *did* boycott grapes for three years.)

Your herbed chicken is renowned; however, on one occasion its piquant flavor is unintentional. It would be wiser *not* to let the guests in on your recipe secret—that the Lawry's Salt you sprinkled on so liberally was not salt. *Don't* explain that your absent-minded son filled an empty Lawry's bottle and neglected to relabel it "Cinnamon Sugar!"

Suppose you are making beef stew and the improbable should happen, because you were too lax to bother recorking. Suppose that, after the stew has begun simmering nicely, you pour the usual swig of red wine from the open bottle—only to discover that some alcoholic mouse squeezed in during the previous night and pickled himself. Do you throw out the stew or do you do a taste test, survive and serve it? If you follow the latter course, and the guests comment on the marvelous, unique flavor, it might be wise just to smile mysteriously.

A Special Place

It HAS BEEN SAID that getting to and from Hanover, New Hampshire, is like climbing up and down Pike's Peak in a Conestoga wagon. This is not true.

It *is* true that before two interstate highways intersected a few miles south of Hanover, driving to Boston took more than four hours while New York City was a good eight hours away—and one had to drive through Albany! Our nearest metropolitan area is Boston; the second is in Canada—Montreal. Amtrak allots us one train a day, but bus service is dependable at all hours in all weather.

In the fifties, the tiny airport serving the Upper Valley had short runways and no tower. Traffic control was the ticket agent who, at the roar of an engine, would desert his customers, don earmuffs, and race out to wave the aircraft in. Now a plucky little airline serves the area with on-time service and a good safety record. We also have longer runways, an air marshal who searches baggage and a traffic control tower with a man in it!

Hanover, which lies on the western edge of New Hampshire and on the bank of the Connecticut is over two hundred years old, with a population of 6500 (without College students). The town measures six by seven miles—a rectangle of twenty-five Central Parks. North is the Presidential Range; west, the Green Mountains of Vermont.

Hanover has two suburbs with much acreage and few people: Small Etna (not named for anything Mediterranean, but from a chance glance at the calendar of the Aetna Insurance Co.) and minute Hanover Center, a center only geographically.

The Green

Although the five-acre Green is owned by Dartmouth College, it is the focus for both town and gown events—planned and unplanned. It sits atop Hanover's main street and business section, which is imaginatively named Main Street.

The Green is criss-crossed with dirt paths which used to turn to swamp-like mud in March. Out came the duck-boards which signaled hope—Spring—and saved many generations from being sucked under. But the duck-boards are gone now, replaced by a better drainage system. Students insisted that the drainage excavations, the long trenches, were really dug to look for a former President's missing College ring.

The Green *is* green in spots not heavily used, trampled upon or torn up by cleats. Turf is consistently being replaced with tougher, more student-resistant grass. One year enterprising undergraduates surreptitiously "improved" the grass seed. When the grass sprouted, so did potato shoots. The remaining very tall trees which ring the Green are elms—survivors of the Dutch elm pestilence. Sprayed, bottle-fed and probably patted occasionally, they stand defiant. The graves of those which succumbed are marked by smaller but hardier maples.

On its four sides the Green is bounded by College buildings. At the southwest corner, one can glide back and forth on the porch of the Hanover Inn, undisturbed, in high-backed cane rockers, lazily watching the happenings on the Green. In time almost anything will happen.

Seasonally there are intramural games—softball, lacrosse, touch football, soccer and snowshoe races.

I remember the last annual tug-of-war between the freshman and sophomore classes. The two-inch-plus rope was long enough to allow the students to abandon the Green and move downtown where all shop doors were tied up and the remainder of the rope was looped around cars and street lamps. That is why it was the last annual tug-of-war.

A major home football game usually means a bonfire, *if* there's enough wood, if it hasn't rained all week and if the wind has died down or the month-long drought is over. Dartmouth bonfires, painstakingly erected by the freshman class in the center of the Green, are not the tepee-type, thrown together. They are a hexagon of railroad ties, tier upon tier, filled with combustibles. The record was set several years ago: over 100 tiers high. That record will stand. "Too dangerous," said the Hanover Fire Department, which always sends a truck to stand by. The freshmen also stand by—all night for several nights—to guard their masterpiece against premeditated, premature lighting.

Hanover children come en masse to bonfires, pockets bulging with horse chestnuts. When heaved into the flames, horse chestnuts explode like cherry bombs. In the good old days, the bonfire was a time to chase unwary freshmen, steal their beanies and scamper off. Our children had a large collection. But beanies are out, and chestnut trees are dwindling.

Ten thousand people throng the Green for the annual "Dartmouth Night." A torchlight parade with bands and a motorcade wends its way through the town to Dartmouth Hall on the eastern edge of the Green; speeches from the steps are broadcast to alumni around the world; and then comes the torching of the bonfire. On a frosty night, after perching uncomfortably on the back of a convertible, I freeze slowly. Trying to control the shakes, I bite my cheeks, hold my knees, tense every muscle, pray for short speeches and a whopping fire. It is either St. Vitus' Dance or pagan fire-worship.

February: the main statue for Winter Carnival in the center of the Green is sculpted, slowly. Progress is dictated by the amount of snow and dependable workers available. Each Carnival has a theme, such as "Through a Frosted Looking Glass" or "The Winterland of Oz." The students outdid themselves on the latter with an ice "Emerald City," lit green at night, with turrets, winding stairs and a long, banked slide from the top. Everyone tried that slide—including the President's wife.

In Spring, or Summer or whenever the snow has disappeared, kites appear. Then come the frisbees chased by people and dogs. The dogs do better.

"Woodsmen's Weekend" follows. Competitors (including women) from colleges all over the East and from Canada come to the Green and set up all types of wooden things which they then try, in record time, to chop up, cut down or saw apart.

Flagpoles on the western side of the Green fly the American flag and Dartmouth's flag; just across the street is the blue banner of the U.N. For a number of years, in weather fair or foul, there was always a small, dedicated group keeping a noon vigil near the flagpoles to protest the war. We were also part of a memorial service held there on the anniversary of the death of Martin Luther King.

The Senior Fence runs under the flagpoles. Supposedly for seniors only, it is a structure to lean against, not sit down on. It is uncomfortable even for lounging. I've tried it.

Commencement is a brilliant flash of color, if the June skies are blue. Academic regalia, summer dresses and the flags of every nation. The seniors march across the Green to the music of Scots Pipers and a brass quintet, flanked by parents, photographers and dogs.

The Green is alive in Summer: Native American "pow-wows" when Indians from all sections of the country join our students in chant and dance; the student-organized and town-sponsored "Summer Carnival"; impromptu and scheduled musical concerts by fiddlers and ballad singers. The Classic Car Club once lined up dozens of magnificent automobiles dating back to 1926. Since I can remember almost all of them, what does that make me?

The town is eight years *older* than Dartmouth and is not hesitant to remind the College of the fact. The town took over the Green to celebrate Hanover's Bicentennial, with speeches, costume parades, band concerts and potato-sack races.

We will miss the student who strolled down the side of the Green each morning playing haunting Baroque melodies on his flute. He has graduated.

Classes are held under the trees on warm days; there are always clusters of students sunning, sleeping—even studying—on the grass. Some space is left for families: parents with picnic baskets and energetic toddlers off their leashes, who spend all *their* time chasing balls or dogs and falling down.

A variety of races have been held on the Green. On the night of the 18th of April in '75 (1975) "Paul Revere" galloped around to alert the town's inhabitants that "The British are coming!" In May "chariot races" are traditional. Each fraternity builds a "chariot." There are three requirements for the vehicle: The container must be manned, it must have wheels and stalwarts must pull it. Rome relived. The race has only one objective: to circle the Green through the gauntlet of cheering bystanders armed with missiles—bags of flour, water guns and an occasional very old egg—without tipping over.

The year I was persuaded by a fraternity to lend my bicycle's red flag on its five-foot pole as a chariot talisman, the chariot crashed. My pole is now *two* feet high.

Two races were not traditional. Professor Maryssa Navarro of the History Department once circled the Green to cheers and was presented with a bouquet of roses from John for her courage. Dressed in full football regalia—uniform, cleats, helmet and cape—she ran to pay off a bet that Dartmouth would not go coed.

A campus streaker once raced diagonally across the Green, which wasn't exactly news. What *was* news was that a student radio reporter kept up with him, mike in hand!

The Campus

The campus is shaped like an open fan with the Green as its handle. The buildings on campus are a conglomeration of two hundred years of changing architectural styles. Some Victorian monstrosities were torn down; several buildings that burned were rebuilt—Dartmouth Hall twice—and finally fireproofed.

The buildings are wine red, pink and whitewashed brick, gray granite, peach limestone, white clapboard, colored tile, poured concrete with the imprint of weathered barnboard. Although they are predominantly Georgian, one can find examples of that post-Civil War period, the Reconstruction. (I wish some *would* be reconstructed.) The Senior Secret Society (Sphinx) holds its meetings in something which can only be described as "Egyptian Tomb period." And we have several examples of Romanesque—ugly.

The Kiewit Computation Center is Greek Revival (circa 1960's); Baker Library resembles Independence Hall, except I doubt that the Philadelphia original ever had its dignified clock face transformed into a Mickey Mouse watch. (Ours did. Its hands wore yellow gloves that circled a smiling mouse for several days.) The facade of the modern Hopkins Center for the Performing Arts resembles the Metropolitan Opera, except that the facade of the Lincoln Center Met was designed by the same architect, later. And I don't believe the Met has ever had to break in and rescue chickens. We have. Cleverly, Dartmouth positioned the student mailboxes in the Arts Center *beyond* the Sculpture Court and galleries. Picking up a letter requires a visual exposure to art. In retaliation, the Sculpture Court, with its trees, grass and abstract sculpture, was transformed one early morning into a padlocked hen-house.

Dartmouth has two nonpillared soaring structures by Nervi and several wooden houses from the eighteenth century. A monstrosity also exists—the smokestack of the College's power plant (early Industrial Revolution). Many have found it an eyesore, especially the class of 1982, which tried to cover it. A very large banner with the class numerals was discovered one Fall morning hanging from the very top, one hundred feet up. The Hanover Fire Department's rescue ladder couldn't save it. And so it remained, a tribute to mountaineering skill.

We have no Gothic edifices. There was once a plan to duplicate the Princeton chapel, which is a copy of the massive one at Cambridge University. I've seen both. In its British setting, the chapel fits quite perfectly in both time and place; in Princeton, the great building is overpowering; at Dartmouth, it would have squashed the campus.

The campus is compact, but the buildings don't crowd. There are green vistas and ivy-covered walls (but no ivory tower). You can walk a bit northeast to the top of Observatory Hill and down to the Bema, a mystical place surrounded by great trees and protected on one side by a 50-foot rocky ledge— a natural amphitheatre. Or walk west past the secluded old Dartmouth Cemetery to the Connecticut River, a quarter of a mile away. Walk east a mile, and you come to Velvet Rocks and the Appalachian Trail; walk north one-half mile out past Occom Pond to the rolling golf course and the great stand of pines; or walk south to Mink Brook less than a mile away—a naturalist's heaven.

Our Town

The town police force is quietly efficient, doesn't overreact to students and manages to keep cool controlling the masses of people who pour into town for Dartmouth events. There were four policemen on the force in 1954; now there are eleven, including two detectives. But felonies and larcenies are up. Interstates bring out-of-towners. More of us lock our doors not only at night, but also during the day. This was unthinkable in the fifties, when we would leave for ten days and forget to lock the front door. Social notes no longer announce a forthcoming trip.

We've gone three decades without a pedestrian fatality. Ninety years have passed since our one and only murder. It began as a typical case—spurned suitor shoots young woman. But its aftermath was atypical. The accused ran off and hid for a month in the barn of the dead girl's family. A mammoth posse searched and peppered the barn with shots. Everyone wanted to get in on the act and did. As a reward, upstanding citizens of the town received a black-edged invitation to the hanging. A most festive occasion.

The town's fire department relies heavily on volunteers— farmers, merchants, faculty members and students. Several Dartmouth students live in. The substation in Etna still relies on about thirty volunteers. The response of both departments is rapid, even if it means careening down vertical drops of ruts and sheer ice, slithering, skidding, almost toppling as the truck roars around the tight curves.

The Dartmouth–Hitchcock Medical Center, a model for rural medical care, treats 300,000 people in an 8000-square-mile area of northern New England. The complex includes M.D.'s and Ph.D.'s doing basic research, a mental health center, the Norris Cotton Cancer Center, open-heart and neurosurgery, nurses who still care and doctors who *will* make house calls.

Dartmouth and Hanover depend on each other; in emergencies they support one another.

When heavy Spring rains caused swollen rivers to overflow, warnings were broadcast that the Connecticut River would crest over flood stage. John ordered dormitories and the dining hall to stand by for possible flood victims. The alert was lifted, but the College had responded.

When a Northeast airliner with forty-two passengers aboard crashed just below the peak of Moose Mountain on the eastern border of Hanover, there were a few survivors and, in the hope that a helicopter could reach them, the Green was transformed. All the heavy trucks from the town and the College formed a wide circle, turned on their motors, switched on their high beams and the Green became a flood-lit landing pad, eerie yet awesome.

When we arrived in 1954, there were no parking meters, no traffic lights, no traffic. We now have an abundance of all three. I resent parking meters and in protest never put in my dime. For years I saved at least ten dollars per annum. Now the police watch for me!

The schools are good and *entirely* supported from property taxes, since the State of New Hampshire—the only state with neither an income nor a sales tax—gives the town zero dollars. New Hampshire has the infamous distinction of being fiftieth in the nation in support of schools.

Hanover and Norwich, Vermont, have the only interstate school district in the country, the Dresden School District. The school is located in Hanover. It was more difficult to organize this district than to work out a treaty with the Soviet Union. Both towns had to approve, as did both state legislatures. The bill went to both Houses of Congress and was signed by the President—one of the last bills ever signed by President Kennedy—in November, 1963. Finally, the pact had to be tested in the Supreme Courts of both states. The Social Security Administration was so confused by the new formation that it wouldn't accept the Social Security taxes. It now treats the Dresden School District as a 51st state!

John was on the School Board during this hectic period. He once pointed out to the two women Board members (out of six) that their combined total of children (12) constituted 1 percent of the school population! Zero Population Growth set up a chapter here soon thereafter.

Town government has changed in some respects since we arrived. Instead of the three selectmen who ran the town, there is now a town manager and five selectmen (two of whom are women). But we still have a Town Meeting where *anyone* can and does speak. "Democracy in the raw" is the usual phrase. Bond issues bring them out from the hills. And in reading the annual Town Report, one can sometimes find something Robert Benchley would have been proud of, such as the recent Animal Control Report. I quote only partially eliminating the references to dogs, cats, raccoons, woodchucks, bats, porcupines and ponies.

Total number of complaints:	*961*
Other animals handled:	*171*
Skunk:	*78* (!) (This is *not* my ex-
clamation point.)	
Miscellaneous animal bites:	*4*
Gerbils:	*1*

Chased home a cow and a calf loose on Goodfellow Road.
Chased two jackasses two miles home on Two Mile Road.
Investigated report of an otter chasing a mailman.

I buy 80 percent of my clothes and almost everything else in Hanover. While the choice is limited, the quality is good. I once scoured Bloomingdale's and much of Manhattan fruitlessly for black sandals, only to find them here on Main Street. True, there is a dearth of exclusive little boutiques, Chateau-Lascombes 1959 and fresh Dover sole, but we survive. The salespeople are friendly and friends. And gift-wrapping is free!

Many say "Hanover" and think of being marooned out in the boondocks. They might have a point if it were only a small, in-bred, northern New England town, but it has a symbiotic relationship with Dartmouth. There is *too* much to do: too many concerts, too many plays, too many guest lectures.

There are adult courses in everything from modern languages and movement, to macrame and meditation. Want to volunteer? There seem to be a thousand chapters of worthy causes just waiting to grab you.

Where else can you have the Chicago Symphony playing, while four miles away black bears roam wild? Not the Chicago Bears! (John's contribution—and his last one!)

I cannot understand those who prefer the city. I suspect they are not comfortable with silence. I suspect their idea of solitude is not wanting to know their neighbors, perhaps because they are uncomfortable with themselves.

The outdoors is a way of life here; too much so, sometimes. A child can learn to ski so well in one year that a mother becomes intimidated. I told my first-graders to shut up and stop yelling from far down the hill, "Come on, Mummy. You're too slow!" Of course I was slow. Side-slipping a slope which they had just schussed took time.

Happily my athletic son didn't learn to skate. Had he excelled, I might have been one of those loving, self-sacrificing parents who chauffeur their child to hockey practice at 5:30 in the morning! Now that I think on it, *my* hockey addict would have had to hike.

The weather is cold for too many months of the year, but the snow does come straight down. We rarely have the winds of Chicago or the blizzards of the Plains. The cold is dry—not damp as in Boston. Many retired alumni settle in Hanover, enduring the winters and the ice, in preference to Phoenix or La Jolla. We do change seasons—sometimes quite beautifully.

Culture and clean water, air that's fit to breathe, green-belt areas, wild areas, zoning that's stiff and taxes that are stiffer—that's Hanover. I miss the loss of fox burrows and grazing cattle. In 1954 there were sixteen farms in operation. They were small, family-run operations, frequently handed down through generations. Small farms make little profit, and today there are only two left.

Friends with young children joined the faculty. They came from a large city where each nice day had been spent on a long journey—taking the children to play in a park. In Hanover they found a house a mile or so from campus. On moving day, the children sat on the front stoop of their new house, bewildered. "Mummy, where's the park?"

"It's all around you."

It's Different at Dartmouth

"IT IS, Sir, as I have said, a small college. And yet there are those who love it. . . ."

Words learned by every high-school student. A major case argued before Chief Justice Marshall and the Supreme Court of the United States in 1818. The College was Dartmouth, and her advocate was Daniel Webster, class of 1801. The College is still small, and still loved—sometimes fiercely—by her alumni, faculty, students, staff, Presidents and first ladies.

And Dartmouth *is* different. Is it the place? The lack of formality and pompousness? Is it the direction the President takes? Is it the basic stuff of the College—her students and faculty? Is it all of these plus a special enthusiasm which sets the College apart and makes her a distinct, very different institution?

Dartmouth in another setting wouldn't be the same. Here there's a freedom beyond the campus bounded only by hills and streams; here there's still a quality of life unspoiled by urban haste and hassle.

The President makes a difference. The College has one who listens, who still pioneers, who unravels complexities and creates imaginative solutions, who will look and plan for the future beyond his own tenure.

Dartmouth is chauvinistic; it is not pompous. It can laugh at itself. Too many institutions take themselves so seriously; if *it* didn't happen on their campus, *it* didn't happen.

The College is comfortable with informality. A President's

wife can disrupt traditions and not be classed an interloper who stepped out of bounds. A student is uninhibited about ringing our doorbell and asking to see the President, for the President is likely to be available. Faculty and administrators are comfortable with friends outside their own departments, outside the academic community. Town and gown communicate.

Dartmouth is not a perfect paradise. Most of her imperfections are quite visible. But a vitality exists here, an optimism that when change is needed, change is possible.

The Students

There is no typical Dartmouth student. They come in all colors from all classes from every state and abroad. I know the daughter of a New York television star and the son of a Beirut taxi-driver. Most are happy here, many are ecstatic, some bitch. Peer pressure is a force for good and bad. Isolation breeds fellowship, spirit and loyalty. It shapes admirable attitudes which last along with some obnoxious macho types which are disappearing. (I will be delighted when the last passes away and is interred.)

The students are bright. If they use their years here well, they graduate with a superb education; if they come only for a good time, they are not here for long.

Physical education is *not* a major, so our athletes are pre-meds and philosophers. A first-string defensive end will have a 4.0 average as a chemistry major and be the valedictorian.

A rural southern black brought to Hanover High School in a program initiated by Dartmouth—A Better Chance—can go on to the College and be called by the English Department "probably the most talented poet ever to graduate from Dartmouth," can become a Rhodes scholar and graduate with honors from Harvard Law School. We remember him, a shy high-school sophomore; we saw him last year, an urbane lawyer.

Seven out of ten undergraduates come from public schools. Half of all students are on financial aid. Dartmouth is one of the few colleges that admits *first* and *then* looks at the family's income. And the College feels it has an obligation to make sure that the student does not have to drop out for financial reasons.

Students are listened to. The administration often adopts suggestions from undergraduates—simple ideas for improving the operation of the College which no one else had thought of.

Students have been told that the faculty are accessible, and they expect them to be. (Many write when they are away at graduate school, or off for a term, how hard it is to see or know a professor.)

Most undergraduates live on or near campus. After a brief era when communing with nature out of town was in, they found that nature was unkind—delivering 35-below temperatures in sparsely heated, rundown farm houses.

The Ivy League's "token black student" of the fifties does not exist anymore. He was one of four or five carefully screened, middle-class applicants. He had to be bright, and he had to "fit in." And then he was homogenized some more. One Ivy League school admitted its first black in 1946, and students burned a cross on campus in protest. Dartmouth admitted its first black in 1824. The token four or five blacks admitted in the fifties have now been replaced by some ninety entering blacks of both sexes—as diverse as the country.

In the 1860's, Nathan Lord, the sixth President of Dartmouth, who held the Fundamentalist view that slavery was ordained by God, refused to confer an honorary degree on President Abraham Lincoln. This action set off a furor which led to Lord's resignation. But it came too late for Lincoln, who was dead before the next Commencement.

In the 1960's, when blacks were being admitted in large numbers to Dartmouth, a request for a house came from the Afro-American Society, and one was found. Whether or not by chance, it was simple justice. The house had once belonged to Nathan Lord.

In 1972, the Dartmouth Plan was devised to utilize the facilities and the calendar for year-round operation. A different plan, a radical change, providing freedom from traditional lock-step modes of education and choice to elect which terms to be on or

off campus. A nine-month break can be taken without delaying
graduation. The summer term is not a frivolous, make-up term;
it has full parity. (What nit-wit thought up this plan? What
idiot made it impossible for the President to take off for a
couple of months during pleasant weather? I am married to
him!)

A junior applied for a job as tour director and got it—on a
Russian cruise ship.

A sophomore completely organized the office of a new eco-
nomic adviser to the President of the United States. When she
returned to Dartmouth, there were wails from Washington:
"We can't do without her!"

Another sophomore recognized a vital need for faster and
better medical service in the New York subway system. He
thought up a plan, went to private and public organizations,
raised the money and financed two vans and twenty police
trained in emergency medical service. He received the first
Civilian of the Year Award from the New York Transit Authority at age 19.

John felt that Dartmouth had an obligation to the American
Indians (or Native Americans, as they rightly prefer to be
called). The College had been founded to educate them, but
few had attended and fewer had graduated. In 1970 Dartmouth
began admitting Mohawk and Sioux, Apache and Cherokee,
Navajo and Eskimo. At first it was rough for the students and
for the College. (A black student from the ghetto, after listening
to a student describing life on the reservation, exploded with
rage: "My God! And I thought we had problems!") Neither
foresaw the complications which came when a naive, frightened
young person was plucked from a reservation and plunked
down in an alien atmosphere. Each year there *is* improvement.
Since 1970, many more Native Americans have graduated from
Dartmouth than graduated in her first two hundred years.

Seventy percent of the entering class arrives on campus two
weeks before College Convocation for the Freshman Trip. You
can spot them immediately; they are the ones bulging with back
packs, weighted down with sleeping bags and frequently wear-

ing pristine, stiff hiking boots. Those who ignored repeated warnings to bring broken-in soft boots will be identifiable later. They are the ones who limp around on crutches, recovering from blisters.

The students leave in small groups with an experienced leader on staggered three-day trips to the White Mountains, hiking, climbing, fishing, bicycling. Almost all the planning, the logistics, is done by upper classmen, many of whom are trip leaders.

There was that Fall when the dean who keeps an eye on such things checked with the organizers at home base in Hanover. "Are you running out of anything?"

"Well . . . no" said the students, puzzled. "But we can't understand the surplus of bread."

Out in the wilderness, the starving groups (our son in one of them) could. They had been provided with ample nourishment —almost. Tins and tins of mayonnaise and meat spreads—and one sole loaf of bread to spread them on.

It is always unwise to underestimate the ingenuity of a Dartmouth undergraduate. We knew him long before he entered Dartmouth—Sidney, a quiet genius. One night 3000 new student mailboxes were installed with combination locks; the next morning 3000 mailboxes gaped wide open. The Dean exploded. "An immoral act!" Not so, said Sidney, very upset. He had figured out 3000 combinations in one evening—*before any mail had been delivered*—to prove that the locks were useless.

As an undergraduate Sidney would play a major role in the development of the Dartmouth Time-Sharing System. And when the computers crashed, he put them back together—outdoing all the specially trained repairmen.

When the Treasurer asked John if he could guarantee the security of the computer system, John was sure that one could be designed so that neither the Director of the Computing Center nor John, himself, could beat it. However, there *was* Sidney. But Sidney had principles and would never abuse his talent.

There are universities where many seniors skip graduation—a ceremony that resembles the production line at General Motors. There can be little pride when, with one incantation, thousands receive the B.A. en masse. (Diplomas may be picked up later at the gym.)

At Dartmouth, Commencement can be moving, diplomas are given out individually and the seniors make it back, even if the trek is difficult.

The June a blond young man introduced himself—"I'm Pete Broberg"—I yelped, for Peter Broberg had two careers: One was finishing up his College courses, which took a bit of juggling; the other was more public. I hardly expected to see him in the reception line; I had seen him only the night before in another line-up—pitching a winning game against the Yankees. But today was important to him. He was a Dartmouth senior about to graduate.

Yearly, the College puts out a Freshman Book, a glossy, small magazine with pictures and short biographical statements from the entering class. Glancing down the columns, one can see bright young faces, proud in high-school graduation portraits, or grinning from informal snaps. A few clowns *will* send in baby pictures, and some will send no picture at all. The year a photo of a deer appeared showed how different Dartmouth is. Can you imagine Harvard admitting a deer? Odes were written extolling the virtues of diversity, sonnets to stags were penned and a column was composed noting that our freshman deer might have a few problems—none of them unsolvable. I've never met our deer; no doubt it is immersed in environmental studies.

I bought a piece of student sculpture for John's birthday. The annual student art show is an event. Hundreds of students enter. With raw wood or metal, oil or paper, hanks of rope or popsicle sticks, they produce exciting art. With good instruction, they discover slumbering talent, which explodes in form and color. My sculpture—large, rounded shapes of polished wood fitted together—was created by a sophomore. I handed him a check for the amount. He handed it right back. If it was for the President, he'd lower the price! I won, citing favoritism. Well, then he'd have to rewax each piece. It must be perfect! He won, and it appeared a week later, gleaming—a labor of love. I lost track of the student until he called one June. He was graduating and his grandfather would be present. Could he bring the elderly man over to the President's House to see the sculpture? Two happy people proudly noted its prominent position in the living room, holding its own among much more expensive *objets d'art*. It is still there.

They came from Bombay on a round-the-world trip, a middle-aged, ebullient Parsee couple who had befriended us in India years ago. In three months they saw and did *everything,* which most of us take a lifetime to merely contemplate. She carried eight washable saris. At Disneyland would you wear silk to slide down the Matterhorn?

Bombay was hot; Hanover was hotter—too hot to cook. We all went to dinner at the Inn, contemplating a lovely view of Baker Tower, softly lit, from the terrace. But finding the perfect view took time. Baker was obscured from some tables, only partially visible from others. We hopped around like pieces on a checkerboard until we were satisfied. Our randomly picked perfect table—four chairs with view—came with a student waiter. Ginger-haired and freckled, big and broad, his accent was pure Boston, until he lapsed into gibberish. We were stunned; our guests weren't. They beamed and chattered back. A young man born and brought up in India usually is fluent in Hindi. Our friends think Hanover is very cosmopolitan, and so it is.

Not all students arrive on campus happily. A freshman from Washington, D.C., arrived by bus, took one look at the College in the country and grabbed the next bus for home. But his mother was unsympathetic and determined. She marched him right back to the bus station and almost immediately he was traveling north again. This time he stayed.

President Hopkins used to go out the back door in the morning so he wouldn't have to step over it.

President Dickey said he could support it or read it—he couldn't do both.

President Kemeny took it in small doses—and sometimes refused to take it at all.

"It" is the "oldest college newspaper in the country" (1799). *The Dartmouth* has been faithful to a tradition of diametrically opposing the viewpoint of the establishment. Its editors, political gadflys and journalistic giants on campus, continue in that vein after graduation. They have become: a satirical film critic, a political columnist, newsmen with clout, politicians with savvy and novelists of realism. On campus they felt they had a duty to be a bit outrageous. Budd Schulberg, an editor in the thirties, took up a just cause of bad labor practices in Vermont, but admitted to me that part of the fun was galling the President.

Undergraduates are young, reporters get carried away, stories are printed out of context, crusades on all things controversial are seized on with enthusiasm and bludgeoned to death—in A+ prose.

But something is happening. In the last several years the typos have been fewer than in *The New York Times,* the stories are more responsible—and accurate. Maybe John will retire *without* a pithy quote about "it."

"Do you know that you have the first black President of the United States at Dartmouth? His name is Michael Hollis—and he's a freshman." John was astonished, but Reg Murphy, the editor of *The Atlanta Constitution,* went on. "Maynard Jackson (then Deputy Mayor) told me he'd have to run for Mayor before Mike graduated."

At an alumni reception that evening several parents came up, among them a Mrs. Hollis. Intrigued, John suggested that Mike drop into the President's Office—sometime. "Sometime" was John's first day back in town.

Mike Hollis grew up in Georgia when blacks still shuffled

into the gutter to avoid jostling a white; when "colored" meant "sit over there" and "don't come in here." But Mike was always a bit ahead of his time. As a small child, he watched his mother drink from the appropriate water fountain. He didn't. He used the one labeled "white," and a white woman helped him reach —taboo for both.

In his high-school years, before he entered Dartmouth on a scholarship in 1971, he had tried more and accomplished more than almost any teenager in the country—black or white. He gathered awards for everything and, in addition, he was elected president of The Atlanta Youth Congress at age 15, won *The Atlanta Journal* Cup as the best all-round senior and represented the State of Georgia as a delegate to the White House Congress on Youth.

He had some spare time. Michael was the first teenager appointed by the Mayor to serve on the board of the Atlanta Children and Youth Services Commission; he wrote sports articles for *The Atlanta Constitution;* worked nearly a year for the Atlanta Braves gathering statistics, writing and doing public relations; and, as a member of the NAACP, he found jobs for unemployed youths.

Then he came to Dartmouth. Earlier, from a foundation grant, John had established student administrative internships in the offices of the President and the Dean of Students to deal primarily with students. (The scope and number have expanded —now there are interns in almost every administrative office from arts to development.) An intern in the President's Office is a liaison between the President and the student body and must be aware of the mood on campus, keeping the lines of communication open. As a sophomore, Mike became John's intern and stayed two years. (A one-year appointment is usual.)

He was always cheerful, bubbling over with a new idea, a possible project. He had a special gift: equal rapport with blacks *and* whites. And he could give an invocation or speech that would knock you out of your chair—a young Martin Luther King.

At Dartmouth he was involved on and off campus. He was a

member of the Afro-American Society, he broadcast sports over
student radio, he was a director of the group that brought outstanding speakers to the College, he maintained the files on all
of Dartmouth's permanent art collections and he spent two
terms abroad in the foreign study program, in Sierra Leone
and France.

He was cited for academic achievement in three courses. (Professors give out *few* citations.) Michael was one of twelve Senior
Fellows, doing an independent thesis, studying the conse-
quences of rapid transit in San Francisco and Atlanta.

During several college Summers, he did some political cam-
paigning. He is always a politician. In March of 1974, he asked
John if he could bring in a friend—a fellow southerner—and
introduce him to the President of Dartmouth. John was booked
at a conference across campus, so it was the office staff, not he,
who met a quite unknown Jimmy Carter two years *before* the
New Hampshire primary.

Two and a half years later, a jubilant Mike Hollis called the
morning after the election from the Atlanta hotel where President-elect Carter was staying to give John some tips on contacts
in the new administration—people to see in the White House.
He was bubbling over again with excitement—and very useful
information.

We keep in touch. Mike just graduated from The University
of Virginia Law School where, not surprisingly, he was President of the Law Student Division (for the United States) of the
American Bar Association. And he was appointed by Chief
Justice Burger as a law student consultant to a special committee studying rules for admission to federal courts. Michael is
now practicing law with an excellent firm in Atlanta.

In the early seventies Reg Murphy wrote an editorial in *The
Atlanta Constitution*. ". . . mark his name down: Michael
Robinson Hollis. The next time you hear it, he may be one of
the candidates for high political office . . . black, smart, ambitious, worldly beyond his years . . . Mike Hollis may well
be standing before this nation describing his vision of what it
could become. . . ."

When Mike reaches that pinnacle—and he will—I'll vote for him. His qualities are many, but two are rare: a true sense of his own worth and a special sweetness.

The Faculty

The attitude of the faculty is different at Dartmouth. Teaching an excited freshman, still open to ideas and not yet veneered with cynicism, is a challenge, not a chore. Excitement is fragile; it needs to be nurtured, not turned off and withered by a bored graduate-student teacher. Most of the nation's universities use graduate students heavily. Cheap labor.

The outstanding researcher who wouldn't know an undergraduate if he bumped into one—who has nightmares about teaching—doesn't belong here. Neither does the teacher whose only piece of research was a Ph.D. thesis.

Putting together a faculty composed of stimulating teachers who also continue doing original work in their field is not easy. The combination is uncommon. Finding professors who feel that an hour spent helping a confused, lost student is not a waste of precious research time, whose first commitment is to their classes, who spend most of their time *on* campus, not *off* touting their achievements and toting up the number of outside consulting jobs, makes recruiting much more difficult. But it can be done.

A faculty member will not get rich on salary. There are children to educate, mortgages to pay off and unbearable property taxes to dig up. Many of the students these professors educate, will, five years out of Dartmouth, be making twice as much as their teachers.

A country that rewards glamour with million-dollar contracts still whines about the modest salary of a professor. "Two courses a term; eight hours of teaching per week! What do they do with all their free time?!"

Dartmouth faculty members spend hours preparing one lecture, they make up and grade their own exams, they read hundreds of papers, they hold office hours for students (and are usually in!), they invite students home, are freshman advisers, serve on College committees and write scholarly books and papers.

And then, if they have free time, they are involved in the region. They are selectmen and Town Meeting moderators, they serve on school boards and recreation councils, they study the environmental impact of industry on the area and they serve in the legislatures of Vermont and New Hampshire.

They are sports fans and sportsmen. They are opera lovers and cellists. They can build a pipe organ or a log cabin. Some live on farms, tend livestock and mammoth gardens, raise their own food and write significant papers on feeding the world.

In 1969 a new kind of chair was established—*not* for research, but to recognize excellence and encourage innovation in teaching. (John was the first recipient.) Dartmouth is primarily an undergraduate institution. Teaching is what it's all about. Sticking out the slow rise to full professor (and only four out of ten assistant professors will make tenure), working hard and saving little, takes a dedicated person. Dartmouth has five hundred.

We've known the professor for twenty years. He revels in teaching and has total recall. Unlike Professor Kingsfield in *The Paper Chase,* he does *not* need a seating chart. He *knows* those 120 faces in the lecture section. Awed students swear he has eyes in the back of his head. Perhaps he does. For fable tells of the time he was standing at the blackboard, writing, when a student sneaked through the back door to his seat, very late. *Without turning around,* the professor boomed out: "So nice to have you join us, Mr. Smith!"

Decades ago another professor was a legend at Dartmouth. Flamboyant and egocentric, he was more easily recognized on campus than the President. And he was particularly proud that he could remember every student he ever taught and when he taught them. While sauntering down the street, he stopped abruptly and triumphantly pointed to a passing gentleman: "Mr. Jones, 1921, second semester, Mechanics 19, row 3, seat 8!"

"You're . . . you're absolutely right!" blurted Mr. Jones. "But who the hell are you?!!"

Dartmouth professors may go to an urban university on sabbatical. They will endure all the outrages of city living, including paying an enormous sum for the privilege of parking in the vicinity of the university—and "vicinity" may mean within a mile radius. They will pay the fee without a peep. Yet, when Dartmouth instituted sticker parking at a modest fee, and the distance from the parking areas to classrooms could be measured in feet, our faculty cried, "Foul!" and "Dartmouth must be different!" The fuss continued for months.

Holidays are ignored by the College. The service staff takes off, but everyone else functions. Classes are held, most offices are humming and John generally has a series of meetings. Even his birthday was not sacrosanct; he was scheduled to chair a meeting of the CAP, which is held every two weeks in the President's Office. The Committee Advisory to the President discusses matters of promotion and tenure. Their debates are serious, in-depth and *very* time consuming. They begin in the middle of the afternoon and *never* end before 6 PM. An earlier adjournment would be certified a miracle.

Before John left that morning I reminded him: It was his birthday, it was the end of May and as usual he was exhausted, he needed some fun. I had planned a modest celebration and they could damn well stop pontificating by 6!

"I can't promise—exactly, but I swear faithfully to be home by 6:30."

He wasn't. He wasn't back at 7. I called the Office. No answer. A ringing phone *could* be heard but was ignored. He wasn't back at 7:30. Fed up and fuming, I gunned my Jeep down Webster Avenue louder and faster than any Porsche. I raced up two flights of stairs, stormed into the meeting, and, quite out of breath, spit out an ultimatum. "You've got five minutes. If you haven't finished by then, you'll have to do without the chairman!"

Mouths dropped. Dead silence. One professor stood up, politely. A lady had entered the room. But I was no lady. I was an avenger who strode haughtily into an outer office and made sure to slam the door.

Four minutes later, the meeting adjourned, all business completed.

There is a formula firmly believed by the faculty which can be written as follows: faculty member = friend; faculty member turned administrator = adversary. Never mind that the faculty member continues to teach; *any* person in the administration is part of the power structure and is immediately suspect.

What happens when one of the most vociferous faculty critics of the power structure, a distinguished senior professor admired by all his colleagues, agrees to take a one-year appointment as a top administrator? Hardly settled into the new job, he is reproached by a good friend from his own department: "You really don't understand the problems of the faculty."

A suggestion: All members of the faculty should be appointed for one year (in lieu of a sabbatical?) to a position in the administration. Some will be valuable, some will be terrible, but all will see a view from *both* sides of the Great Divide.

In 1971 a stir began on campus, grew into a rumpus and ended in a great debate dubbed—unofficially—"The Mrs. Kemeny Case." Why? I had gone to a faculty meeting.

I went to learn, not to unhinge the faculty. I wasn't a feminist trying to crash an almost exclusively men's club; I went as the President's wife who had become a nationwide spokesman for the College. I needed to know Dartmouth's problems and the direction she was taking. I went to save my husband valuable time. Why should he have to regurgitate a three-hour meeting when I could brief myself?

Attendance at these meetings was confined to the Arts and Sciences faculty, senior administrators (who felt free to send a *very* junior administrator in their place) and representatives from the student newspaper and radio station. Wasn't I as necessary to the College as some administrators? Shouldn't I have as much access as the student media? I poured out these arguments to John who agreed, "Why don't you come." I did. I sat quietly in the back, absorbed, and didn't even interrupt.

I was not unnoticed. A delegation of senior faculty soon confronted John with an enormous problem: "Unauthorized persons are attending faculty meetings!" My name was not mentioned. John didn't bristle; he listened calmly and then informed the group that the "problem" would be brought before the Executive Committee.

Was there anything in the Faculty Handbook to cover this situation? John couldn't find a definitive statement. Although the rules were explicit about who could *vote* in faculty meetings, nowhere did they state who could *attend*. The Executive Committee chewed on the "problem," trying to find some guidance in the rules. They failed, so the matter was sent on to the Committee on Organization and Policy. And here the debate ended. For the elected chairman that year was a populist social scientist who took a very far-out position. Not only should Mrs. Kemeny have the right to attend meetings of the faculty— meetings should be open to *all* members of the Dartmouth community (even students!). And this view carried.

Now, in the Observer Section (marked by a handsome card), sit faculty spouses, students, staff, townspeople and me—all "unauthorized persons" a few years ago. No one checks our credentials. Fifty to a hundred will come if the agenda is likely to be controversial; more often there are only ten. The visitors listen politely. There are no demonstrations or giggles.

And probably most of the faculty don't even remember the time when they were whispering, "My God! The President's wife! It isn't done!"

We roar out of Paris at dawn in a car driven by a Gallic terror who's really Greek. Hurtling towards the Loire Valley, we are trapped and must comply. The demand is awful. Before the day is over we *will* give speeches to the mayors of two cities—in French. I pray for the day to be over. My French, always atrocious, is rusted and decayed, and was never recycled!

But Dartmouth Professor John Rassias is persuasive. He is the driver. In the back seat I practice the short speech he has prepared. I have to do well, for as the narrow two-laned road

twists and turns, so does Rassias—a 180-degree turn of his body
to correct every mistake. I can tell when my pronunciation
grates: His foot jerks in pain—down on the accelerator.

Sixty percent of all Dartmouth students take one or more
terms abroad in twenty language-study and foreign-study centers—probably the most extensive program in existence. Our
trip will be a day-long site visit to two of Dartmouth's language
centers in Bourges and Blois. We are supposed to experience
the students' fluency in French, not worry about ours!

But John Rassias is indefatigable. A man who chain-smokes
as he chain-speaks, this Romance Language Professor is part
actor, part dynamo, all teacher. (He was honored as one of the
ten most gifted teachers in the country a few years ago.) He has
revolutionized the teaching of languages with a method he invented for Peace Corps trainees. With swarthy, mobile features,
sharp black eyes and masses of dark hair always in disarray, he
could be a Mediterranean brigand. His hair gleams from the
sweat of exertion. Grimacing, he works with a student to pull
out not just the exact phrase, but the perfect inflection, rhythm
and pronunciation. With success, the grimace turns to grin of
demonic glee.

The brigand is grinning now. We have arrived *on the dot* in
Bourges. Infuriating! We are whisked—time is not to be wasted
—to meet Dartmouth's French liaison. Hallelujah! English
spoken here. I take some Perrier water. Then on to luncheon
in a secluded old mill. A simple country restaurant: lobster
quenelles, wild mushrooms, pineapple Chantilly and lots of
Sancerre. *"Merveillieux"* is a marvelous word to be used over
and over. Covers a lot of sins. We give our speeches, the French
officials nod happily, applaud politely and don't wince once
(diplomats).

No time to digest. The Dartmouth students are ready to feed
us again! They have been here one month, having had either
high-school French or a seven-week's intensive French course at
the College before flying over for the three-month term. They
are immersed in the language. Their host families speak no
English; most students "go home" to lunch, the main meal of

the day; so all phrases pertaining to eating must be learned rapidly—particularly "Repass the wine, please." Students confide that wine at lunch makes learning in the afternoon a disaster.

Now the drill session. The students sit in a semi-circle, and Rassias does his stuff. His entire body is in motion. The question cracks. Randomly the finger points and snaps—the answer, the answer! Around the room, never stopping: question—answer! His hands are a blur. His face is contorted with pain or pleasure. Pulling, tugging, drawing out—rhythm, recitation, repetition, retention: his four R's. (The French speak three times faster than Americans, he says. I thought it was ten times!) Just speak, speak! Don't think, don't grope. Spit it out. Right! *"Très bien, monsieur."* Wrong. Snap, snap. Someone else is ready to give the correct reply, you will be corrected instantly—and *that* mistake won't be made again!

One month and those students are articulate and uninhibited. The drill sessions resurrect my third-grade teacher thrusting a pointer under my nose and commanding "9 $\times$ 7!" I stammer when pointed at. I'll have to learn French another way.

There's just time for a quick tour of the Bourges Cathedral. A Judas tree close by is in pink blossom. Mammoth, misty in the slight drizzle, the cathedral's stained glass is said to rival Chartres. But we have a schedule to keep and no time to compare. Rassias hustles us to the car, for he has a rendezvous with the French liaison on the outskirts of Blois who will show us an intricate short-cut into the city. Watch for a lone man in a small blue Renault parked on a wide shoulder x kilometers from Blois. We spot him. Rassias swears. Thirty seconds late!

Halting pleasantries with the Frenchman and his family at home. No English spoken here. More Perrier water. I am awash. I attempt a more meaningful conversation which involves my pregnant cat. I can't remember the French word for "pregnant." I draw pictures in the air. I am *not* coming across! Why the hell did I begin this conversation? My French, unlike old burgundy, does *not* improve with age. It also does not travel well.

We're off to a large reception held in our honor. Formally, the Dartmouth students of Blois introduce us to their families —to *"ma mère et mon père."* *"Enchanté,"* dredged from my subconscious, is another useful word to cover contingencies. More food, a lot more wine. Thank God for Perrier water! There are speeches to us in French from the city officials, speeches from us to the officials in more or less the same language. Presents and toasts are exchanged. How will I pack the presents? How will I pack more liquid into me?! The students sing "Men of Dartmouth" in impeccable French—and completely off key. Great rapport. Once the French get used to the informality and openness of American teenagers, relations are warm. A young black student, who broke his leg on his first day, is hovered over by his French family and endearingly called *"bébé."* I do discover one unhappy student. His French is still halting, for he had been placed with a kindly old spinster whose only topic of conversation is her pet parakeet. There is just so much one can discuss about parakeets in halting French.

Very, very late at night we start back to Paris. Paris to Bourges to Blois to Paris—three hundred miles. We stop in Orléans for coffee. I feel as martyred as Joan of Arc, until I look at Rassias and feel much better. He is exhausted!

"The Granite of New Hampshire
Is Made Part of Them 'til Death"

TAKE 40,000 people, still mostly male, scatter them around the world in over one hundred countries, territories and islands and they will find each other. China, 1945: A Jeepful of soldiers singing at the top of their lungs is racing unknowingly towards Japanese lines. In No-Man's Land they are halted by an MP who gives them hell and "Was that 'Men of Dartmouth'?" Then holding out his hand he introduces himself as X of the class of—. Naturally, the Jeep acquires a formidable motorcycle escort back to safety.

The ties are strong, the bonds unbreakable. With a few exceptions—the obstreperous, the crass, the narrow-minded—Dartmouth alumni are the most loyal and supportive group of *any* institution in the country. They give money, a lot of it, to the College. But they also give time, an immense amount of it, to Dartmouth, free.

They try to find the best high-school students and encourage them to apply. Each applicant is interviewed by an alumnus; that will be over 8000 interviews for an entering class. They find interim jobs for undergraduates and full-time ones for graduates. Four seniors on a cross-country bike tour were hit by a truck and severely injured. Alumni rallied to help.

Good legal advice is always available. The alumni lobby with the federal government against idiotic and conflicting laws that seriously affect the College. They serve on College committees willingly. A high-ranking judge, living a considerable distance from Hanover, was asked by John to serve on a special committee. His answer: "Mr. President, when the court sits, I have to be here. Any other time I *will* be there."

Alumni relations are a major part of the job of the President (and the President's wife). Good communication, rapport and understanding between the alumni and the College are, in the end, up to us. And they are terribly necessary.

During the student uprisings in the late 1960's almost every college admissions office reverberated with cries from irate alumni. "How could you have admitted all those trouble-makers? You're obviously using the wrong criteria!"

But at Dartmouth, when a group similarly outraged tried to second-guess the Director of Admissions, he didn't argue: "All right, gentlemen. *You* are now the Committee on Admissions. Here are fifty student folders with only the names excised. Each folder contains *everything* we knew about the candidate. From those fifty we picked twenty. Now you are on your own to do the same."

The alumni, after hours of discussion, proudly presented their choices. They had "admitted" an outstanding scholar–athlete, the editor of *The Dartmouth,* the head of the SDS (the Students for a Democratic Society) and several other students who organized the takeover of the administration building!

In John's first year as President an alumnus from the Midwest wrote a bitter letter complaining that the local alumni group, of which he was a member, had scheduled a function at a private club which the alumnus could not join because he was a Jew. John immediately laid down an edict that no official Dartmouth alumni function would take place in a facility that barred membership because of race or religion. There may have been convulsions, but the edict stood and the alumni cooperated.

A year later, an officer of the College came to John with a

problem. While the alumni had agreed to hold a banquet in a facility with no restrictive membership rules, one alumnus with long ties to a venerable men's club wanted very much to hold a small private luncheon in John's honor. That club *did have* discriminatory clauses. Could John make an exception?

My husband replied, "But what if the club won't let *me* in?"

A happier story: An alumnus from a city steeped in history and culture planned a luncheon for John. This time the man had already made the arrangements at his private club before the Dartmouth Alumni Office had checked for discriminatory clauses. The alumnus, a distinguished and thoughtful person, rechecked and found that there were clauses—no Jews or blacks. Hastily the luncheon was rescheduled to a much less attractive facility.

Recently, the alumnus called John to invite him to luncheon at that same private club: "I think you'll find some changes." Because of my husband's earlier action, the alumnus and several friends decided that something had to be done about bigotry; so together they had successfully managed to throw out the discriminatory membership rules.

Not all alumni are so flexible; some have no understanding. An alumnus and his wife were at a small reception with us. Their only topic of conversation was a faculty member's suit. It was rumpled; they were also sure that the back of his collar was frayed. And didn't he have a spot on his tie? I explained that the faculty member was a kind and brilliant man, a fine teacher who does nationally respected research and who could make double his salary in industry. The couple refused to listen and ignored my list of his qualities. Next they were sure he was missing a button on his jacket.

They will not be invited again.

A warm and quite marvelous alumnus sat next to me at a dinner in his honor. The honor was an endowed chair in his name donated by friends and several corporations. There was obviously something on his mind. "She was with me all the way. I couldn't have done it without her. Do you think I could add her name to the chair?"

"It's a beautiful idea. Do it."

And he did, immediately. His wife's name was added, discombobulating several administrators who had all the press releases ready—with only one name on them.

And then there was the alumnus who wrote my husband suggesting that he would be "a damn good President of the United States!" John wrote back thanking the man, but pointing out that he was not eligible. Although he was now a United States citizen, he had been born in Hungary, and the Constitution does not allow a naturalized citizen to be President. The alumnus wrote back: "I think I'll sponsor a bill in Congress to get the Constitution changed."

I remember our first alumni swing to the West Coast. Student unrest and anti-war protests were to reach a convulsive climax the following month in reaction to Kent State and Cambodia.

Paranoia ran rampant in California. The first demonstrations had begun there at Berkeley, followed by Haight-Ashbury, San Francisco State, the Manson cult. To a large segment, bare feet and long hair meant drugs, free sex and revolution.

The pre-banquet alumni cocktail party was held in a spiffy hotel with a good turnout to meet the new President of Dartmouth and his wife. And, as at any alumni function, invitations were sent to undergraduates who were in the area. Many of these students had taken a term away from campus to work at one of the College's off-campus programs, located in ghetto areas or Indian reservations around the country.

Most of the alumni were dressed to the teeth; the students were not. They had come straight from the ghetto. They were clean, wore shoes and a jacket, but they had long hair—at least down to their collars. (Three-piece suits and a semi-monthly visit to the barber are not requirements for tutoring children who are poor and black.) These young men were stereotyped from the beginning.

Several alumni, still smarting from the "student troubles" and possibly fearful of more to come, began making the inevitable remarks about hair length and hippie types. As the remarks grew louder and more pointed, I became angry. Grabbing a student, I pulled him over to one of the noisier alumni. Gloatingly, I introduced them: "Mr. X, I'd like you to meet one of our undergraduates who has left a cloistered environment in Hanover to try to help in *your* ghetto area. He's co-captain of the Dartmouth Ivy Champion football team!" That football player was back for his fifth reunion and is now a major force in his class. The older alumnus? He probably wears *his* hair long now—perhaps curling over the collar.

Dartmouth alumni have the resiliency to bounce back when an unpopular decision is made at Dartmouth. They explode, feel better and then live with the decision. And most come to accept inevitable change.

In the Fall of 1971 the Trustees voted to admit the first undergraduate women in the two-hundred-year history of Dartmouth. In the several years following, resistance to the decision subsided. The Great Debate was over. At least, so John thought, when he accepted an invitation to lunch in a southern city not known for its liberalism. His host, an alumnus with a long and active career in alumni affairs, opened the conversation abruptly: "My two sons and I went to Dartmouth. For years, the three of us have worked hard for her. But when the Trustees voted to make the College coed, we decided to have nothing more to do with Dartmouth!" John lost his voice; he almost lost his lunch. The alumnus, relishing the moment, paused interminably before continuing: "On the other hand, my daughter—a sophomore at Dartmouth—has shown us the error of our ways!"

The alumni who rebel against change in their College remind me of a story of an earlier group of dissident graduates. When running water was installed in the dormitories the alumni howled: "We fetched our own. This luxury will breed generations of sissies, destroy the character of the College and Dartmouth men will no longer be men!"

The farther one travels from the seat of action, the more one finds the attitude of alumni changing. If a topic such as the ratio of men to women, the reinstitution of ROTC or bringing back the Indian symbol is discussed, the group in Hanover and environs will rage, the North Shore of Boston will growl, San Francisco will be unconcerned and Hawaii will say, "What's all the fuss about?"

It's a good day when an alumnus comes up to us and says, almost with tears in his eyes, "You two are doing a hell of a job. We're with you all the way!" Or when an alumnus writes, "Take care of each other, for we all need you both." It helps to make up for the few stinkers.

A Very Special Alumnus

J. Clarence Davies, Dartmouth, 1934. I never knew what the J stood for. It seems practically no one else knows either. I never checked his total monetary giving to Dartmouth. I never asked him his party or his politics. But I'm sure he wouldn't have voted for any regressive measures on anything.

Long before I knew Clarence, his son Alan and I were friends—having met on the stage in the 1962 Dartmouth Players production of *Li'l Abner*. As scantily clad Dogpatch inhabitants, we hammed and pranced, tippling from my ever-present jug. (Faculty wives were in great demand to play female roles then. With coeducation, we have been supplanted by much younger, and more talented, Dartmouth women.)

Clarence was a contradiction. A rabid alumnus who never missed a home football game, he was *not* the rah-rah type who wanted the College to return to the nineteenth century. He was famous for his treks to Hanover. Arriving on Friday afternoon with his wife, Helen, he'd stay the weekend, going to all possible sporting events and any scheduled meetings. She had a bad back and frequently would do the entire trip lying down, but not as a martyr, for she loved Dartmouth and football as much as Clarence. They met at Green Key Weekend in Clarence's freshman year, were engaged by the end of his sophomore year, married after his last exam and interrupted their honeymoon to come back for graduation. While Clarence never missed a football game, he also never missed a chance to push for change in the College when he felt it was needed. He supported co-education heartily.

In World War II he commanded fighter and service wings over Europe and later was commissioned a major-general in the Air Force Reserve. I couldn't believe he was a general. He was so unlike my stereotype of the rigid, narrow, military mind. Yet he loved the military and defended it. And that made him a key person on a committee of conservatives and radicals to study the possibility of Dartmouth's reinstituting ROTC. He gained the respect and praise of both sides.

He was an enthusiastic person, who never lost his enthusiasm for the College. When he was picked to be on the Alumni Council, he felt it was an enormous honor. He made every meeting until his death.

His nickname was a very unmilitary "Peanuts," given to him long before the cartoon strip was invented. He *was* short, several inches shorter than I. Yet he loved and excelled in sports all his life. At Dartmouth he was light-weight boxing champion. In later years, tennis became a passion. He not only played it, he also became head umpire of the American Lawn Tennis Association, officiating at Forest Hills and at Davis Cup matches.

He always gave so much of himself. His time given to Dartmouth, to the City of New York and to charitable institutions was real time and hard work. He didn't collect honorary titles.

He raised money for Dartmouth as a class agent, frequently a thankless job. He interviewed students as a member of the enrollment committee. He also served on the boards of at least twenty civic, charitable and professional organizations. He was chairman of New York City's Bicentennial Program and, as a classmate wrote, "despite crippling budget cuts was largely responsible for the city's memorable July 4th celebration, right down to the fireworks. . . ."

A warm man, he seemed to laugh a lot. He gave us a boost when we were low. More than once he lifted our morale when we needed support or a friendly word. When some of his contemporaries were bitching, Clarence was bolstering. When he said we were doing a good job, we knew we were. When he was proud of the direction Dartmouth was going, we knew we were on the right track.

The day I saw Clarence Davies' picture on the obituary page of *The New York Times* was a day of blue funk. It must have been so for many others: Co-workers, employees, associates—all friends—inserted more messages of sympathy and sorrow into the death notices than I can ever remember seeing for people infinitely more wealthy, famous or supposedly beloved.

Money, Money. Who's Got the Money?

The yearly Dartmouth Alumni Fund is the life-support system of the College—free funds to be spent as needed. Since 1970, when John became President, the goal has increased from two million to more than five million, and each year the Fund has gone over the top. All this in spite of student turmoil, some dissatisfaction with College policy, inflation, recession and a stagnant stock market. Dartmouth has always surpassed Harvard and Yale in individual participation and runs a close yearly race with Princeton. I suggested that John spell out to the alumni what these free funds really mean: They exceed the income from one hundred million dollars of endowment!

We have few of the very wealthy, very disenchanted and very powerful alumni that Yale and Princeton battle. (See "Annals of Higher Education" by E. J. Kahn, Jr., in *The New Yorker*, May 23rd, 1977.) We don't have alumni who tell industry *not* to give to an institution unless it has looked into the classroom and approved of what is being taught there.

We do have some alumni who could make the difference—

the margin that would solve the constant battle of the budget—but won't. There is one extremely wealthy alumnus who won't support his College because the faculty teaches such radical ideas as that every human being has a right to food, clothing and shelter.

I have met an alumni wife wearing several large emeralds and a tiger coat, both genuine, and listened to her husband plead poverty. He is not in hock. He is a skinflint. He helped to wipe out tigers, but he won't help to wipe out a deficit.

We have a smattering of these types. They do little overt damage. It's what they don't do that hurts.

But there's another type. He doesn't require stroking. He hates to be courted, wooed or kowtowed to; he cannot solve all the problems of the College, but would like to. His donations have no strings attached; yet after several very large gifts, he will come back and say, "Tell me what else you need."

There is also the strapped alumnus who doubles his Dartmouth Alumni Fund gift because, "I want to help this generation of Dartmouth students get the same quality education I had . . . something that will always be very precious. . . ."

There is the parent of an alumnus who gave $1000, which he could not afford, when his grandson graduated.

There is the man who began in the Tuck Business School at age 49 and graduated last year. He made a gift to Tuck School and also one to the undergraduate College, "Because of the wonderful sense of community. . . ."

This type of alumnus far outnumbers the other kind.

Fourteen Special Alumni

All universities are governed by boards—regents, state legislatures, trustees. They have the final say over the allocation and expenditure of funds, the running of the institution. They also hire and fire the president. Regents can be overbearing and undereducated; legislative bodies are frequently long-winded and short-sighted; certain boards of trustees have a men's club mentality, austere and elitist.

Not so the Dartmouth Board of Trustees. They are not a remote body on some unreachable higher plane making decisions
in a vacuum. They work, they really work, learning and understanding. They know the problems, from the broad ones of the
entire College to those of the faculty and the students, and they
know them first-hand.

The Dartmouth Board is small—fourteen members. All are
male (though I suspect there will be a woman soon); all are
Dartmouth alumni. The incumbent Governor of New Hampshire and the President of the College are ex-officio members.
The Board meets officially five times a year for several days, and
each Trustee has a number of separate committee assignments.
Rarely does a member miss a meeting. They arrive in blizzards
and sometimes sneak out of hospitals illegally to make a meeting. A Trustee, dying of cancer, insisted that he had to be present to toast John as President-elect. And he was.

The Dartmouth Trustees are compatible and relaxed, with a
sense of perspective and a sense of humor.

When the Board elected John, they did not realize that they
were electing a night owl—that the usual 8 AM meeting start
would have to be moved up to 9 AM. John does not function
at 8. He rarely functions any better at 9 and drags in late. The
day he arrived on the dot was so unprecedented that the Board
rose as one to give him a standing ovation.

My husband is evaluated each year—to keep or not to keep.
The Chairman summoned him to say that he had a job for another year. ". . . It is the unanimous decision of the Board
that you are a superb President—after 9:30 in the morning."

For some presidents' wives the relationship to governing
boards is an adversary one, ranging from a fight for a desperately needed expense account to a fear of candor: ". . . I keep
my mouth shut. I don't want to jeopardize my husband's career."

If my husband's career depended on a close-mouthed wife, he
would have been fired immediately. The Republicans on the
Board accept my vocal Democratic partisanship. I try to convert.
One even stayed up until 3 AM with me to watch McGovern's

acceptance speech. (If he had ever thought of voting Democratic that year, which I doubt, the loss of sleep undoubtedly threw him back into the Republican camp.)

After a day of meetings, there is a fight—John and three Trustees are fiendishly playing dominos. Across the room two Board members are jazzing it up on the piano as some of us sing along.

I serve them dinner several times a year. A Hungarian meal was particularly popular—so much so that one Trustee asked for an extra piece of a rum cream torte to take home to the Midwest. He would preserve it overnight on the frigid window sill of the Hanover Inn. His wife won't let him forget that he left it there.

Many Trustees are sensitive to and understand my frustrations as the wife of the President. I certainly voice them enough. But they are supporters, and they are my friends.

I have found a marvelous way to travel quickly, if not painlessly. This method eliminates carrying heavy bags, traipsing long corridors and all bureaucratic red tape: Pop your back out. But be sure to do it in Denver, for Denver is an enclave of loyal, sympathetic and very helpful Dartmouth alumni.

Trying to build a stone wall, tossing heavy rocks around as though they were tennis balls *and* pulling up recalcitrant raspberry bushes for two days was showing off and stupid. I paid for it the following week, 2000 miles from home. Brushing my teeth, I coughed, a gentle little cough—and all hell broke loose. Agony.

A lawyer/Trustee recommended an orthopedic surgeon. A pediatrician set up an immediate appointment at the emergency room. The surgeon squeezed me in between examining the Denver Broncos. The following day a Cadillac dealer took full charge: He whisked me to the airport, picked up my ticket, arranged for an electric car (with a cowboy driver), produced a stiff drink and had me escorted on the plane before the other passengers.

All four men were Dartmouth alumni.

Waiting for me in Boston was a College car, driver, pillows and a blanket. Ruth LaBombard, John's assistant, had also been busy.

It's frightening to become incapacitated far from home. But I will remember the entire incident as one not of pain, but of great kindness, and a hell of a good way to get home in a hurry.

June, 1978: Another reunion banquet. Another dais. A twenty-fifth reunion banquet. (These always run on and on—three or four hours of speeches, camaraderie, awards, speeches, reminiscences, jokes, slide-shows, singing and speeches.) My ninth twenty-fifth reunion banquet. Nine times four equals thirty-six hours of twenty-fifths!

This year's banquet promises to be very long. A distinguished class, an exuberant one—the class of 1953. Rightly exuberant. They have just raised one million and fifty-three dollars for the College—by far the highest total any class has ever pledged to Dartmouth. They plan to celebrate. With no forewarning, I will add to the length of the evening.

It is late, my shoulders ache. (Good posture before half a thousand people becomes a pain after three hours.) I am only half listening as the president of the class rises to extoll someone else. Background, accomplishments, personal things. The phrases wash over me. Then I begin to listen, understand and burst into tears as the president reads a resolution from the class of 1953:

> WHEREAS Jean Alexander Kemeny has rendered great service to all the classes of Dartmouth College . . .
>
> WHEREAS Jean Alexander Kemeny's service as Dartmouth's first lady has brought unique distinction to herself, our College and her marriage . . .
>
> NOW THEREFORE, the class of 1953 of Dartmouth College does . . . hereby adopt Jean Alexander Kemeny as a member of the class . . . and does further declare that (she) shall henceforth be a member of the class of 1953 for life . . . to receive and enjoy all the rights, privileges and benefits of membership in the world-wide fellowship of Dartmouth alumni.
>
> June 17, 1978.

The class of 1953, 684 men—and now one woman.

But what will the older classes think? In polls they had been less than enthusiastic about admitting women to Dartmouth. Several months later I am in northern Vermont to give a short talk to a group of Rotarians. Dartmouth alumni in the area have also been invited. There is the suggestion that the Dartmouth guests stand, introduce themselves and give their class. Six or seven rise. Then a query from one alumnus, class of 1929: "And isn't there a representative from the class of '53 here?" A long pause as we scan the room. Have I missed someone? And then it hits. Me! I bounce up to stand with the others.

True acceptance.

Family in a Fishbowl

A SHORT, DIGNIFIED ceremony can instantly change one's way of life. Our family, known but not stared at, has become an object of curiosity and *is* stared at. It is unpleasant under glass.

At any gathering, small or very large, it is certain that we will not know everyone. It is also certain that everyone will know us. Reaching this high plateau automatically makes us experts on any subject or issue—from orchids, antiques, icons and chamber music, to the future of mankind.

What can't be seen is surmised and what is surmised is wafted as rumor and then established as fact. For example: The Kemenys do not live in the President's House. They have never lived in the President's House. They live in a small house in Lyme. (This "fact" circulated for five years *before* we bought a small house in rural Hanover.)

We are fair game for gossip, usually not malicious. My hairdos and clothing styles are scrutinized; so are the children's modes of life. Our every pronouncement seems fascinating and full of import, and is commented upon—frequently backwards, out of context.

To a certain segment, even my daily schedule seems terribly interesting. Do I take a nap in the afternoon? (God, yes, if there's time.) Do I rise briskly at the crack of dawn? (Never—I rise *very* slowly. I am foul tempered in the morning, and will kill anyone who cheerily chirps, "Cherries are ripe!") At what hour do I retire? (As late as possible: 3 AM if I have a good book.)

The only way to survive this glass bowl existence is to conjure up delightful ways to shock. And then don't use them. Nine-tenths of the fun is in the plotting.

Every public stand will be unpopular with someone or some group. The person who should take a public stand but says least has the fewest detractors. That person is also a blob.

I'm excluding Walter Cronkite here. (Although sometimes when he comes home from the evening news his wife, Betsy, will chastise him gently for not speaking out more.) His strength lies in his impartiality on the air. About the time they were our house guests for a weekend, a national poll was published showing that Cronkite was "the most trusted person in the country." So I asked an obvious question, "With that following, why don't you run for political office?" A paraphrase of his answer: "My following *now* is for being an impartial newscaster. If I ran for office, I would and should take a firm, public stand. Then watch how quickly my following would shrink."

That phrase from *Exodus*, "The sins of the father are visited upon the children," could be rephrased. "The imagined sins of a public figure are visited upon his family."

Two examples of this truth come from political families close to us: The first is that of a state Senator in another part of the country. He was a prime mover of a very controversial, progressive piece of legislation. It became law, but not before a number of fanatical attacks from the Right. His house was picketed; the family received nasty phone calls; the children were harrassed at school. Because of the Senator's education committee chairmanship, his wife's application for a teaching job was turned down flatly by a school—for "*we* know you only want to spy."

The second example was a vicious attempt by a Neanderthal newspaper publisher to smear a political enemy. In a series of articles he played up an innocuous remark on marijuana made by the official's sixteen-year-old daughter. By brutally twisting those remarks, the publisher did succeed in hurting the father: The child had a nervous breakdown.

I have read nationally circulated stories about other college presidents' children picked up on a drug charge (usually marijuana), or involved in an automobile accident when neither drinking nor carelessness was the charge. It mattered not that the story was anticlimactic; the family's name was news.

We've been lucky. The children have tried pot; they each have had one minor automobile mishap. None of those incidents made the papers. But Jenny's involvement with a small-town lynch-mob mentality did. And it didn't happen in Dixie. During that week of Kent State–Cambodia, Jenny joined a group of Dartmouth students to gather signatures on petitions for ending the Vietnam War. In a small town they noticed that their car was being followed by a group of New Hampshire rednecks in a pickup. One Dartmouth boy found refuge in a house, another had his glasses broken and a third was beaten up. Jenny speeded them to the town's police station; the police were not terribly sympathetic. The story headlining Jenny as the daughter of the President of Dartmouth made some New Hampshire papers. One alumnus was outraged, not at the treatment of the students, but that a member of the President's family could be involved in such a fracas.

What is the roughest part of being a member of the family of a public figure? Living up to an image? Spending much of your time in public—on view? Lack of privacy? Worrying about your actions being misconstrued? None of the above. It's the unjust criticism sometimes thrown at John that both the children and I detest. It's bad for the psyche to control one's temper —it's worse for the stomach. Therefore, in private, I knock off heads at night; write scathing letters and don't send them (although I did once—to *The Dartmouth,* accusing them of scurrilous journalism); yell loudly and throw things—in the House. Constant public eruptions lose their effectiveness. I save the big public blow for momentous occasions—and then I'm a volcano! Every two or three years is my rule.

Two Special Alumni

Jenny and Rob have a very mixed, but fascinating, heritage, which makes them interesting and creative people.

Their ancestors include two Governors of Massachusetts three hundred years apart; a great-great-grandfather who fought at Gettysburg; a Hungarian–Jewish drummer boy in the 1848 Revolution. A several times great-grandfather was a member of Rogers' Rangers; their great-grandfather was brought up in a brownstone in New York City in the era and tradition of "Life with Father." Clarence Day was his cousin. They had a grandfather who was a Hungarian cavalry officer and fought for the Kaiser and a great-uncle who was a medic in the same war but on the opposite side. They had an ancestor who marched from Londonderry, New Hampshire, to Bunker Hill, and another, a federal judge, who was impeached and found *guilty* by the United States Senate—the first such guilty verdict in the country. They had a great-grandfather who was a druggist in St. Albans, Vermont, and died of a heart attack at the age of 56 at home; they also had a great-grandfather who was a bank teller in Budapest and was murdered at the age of 75 at Auschwitz.

The children were young teenagers at the height of adolescence when their father became President. They had identity crises, emotional upheavals. As children they had problems; as a family we had problems. There were long conversations, much rooting to get to the nub of the unhappiness and much effort trying to cope with life in a fishbowl.

We learned much from them. They made us take a second look at our cherished, but sometimes stagnant, values; having teenagers of our own made it easier to understand Dartmouth students. And having both children attend Dartmouth gave us insight and feedback that we would never have gotten any other way.

Jenny began college at another institution but decided to transfer to Dartmouth in her sophomore year. Rob was accepted at the three colleges he had applied to, but chose Dartmouth. Neither child had a brilliant career at the College. They were as lazy and as hard-working as many of their peers. They procrastinated, went through periods of low motivation and against all parental advice (or because of it) skipped classes and crammed all night for exams. Looking back, both children

would like to redo certain portions of their Dartmouth careers
—variations on a theme we have heard from hundreds of students.

The children had one handicap: They were our children,
the children of the President. The faculty said: "This is not
what I would expect from the President's child," or "I would
have expected more from a Kemeny." Once, Rob, fed up with
the "Kemeny" expectations, suggested that a professor reread a
paper and "Think of it as being written by 'just plain Rob'."

Both children were accepted—up to a point—by their peers
at Dartmouth. Rob, more than Jenny, because he made more
of an effort. But any acceptance took twice as much effort. They
never quite overcame the handicap of visibility.

Jenny was upset by an incident on campus and wrote a furious letter to *The Dartmouth*. But she felt that her protest had
more clout unsigned, and asked that her name be withheld. She
says:

> . . . If Daddy was doing something which was in any way un-
> popular, no one was going to believe that I could possibly
> present an unbiased view of the situation. They didn't under-
> stand the kind of a person my father was—that he always told
> the truth to us. However, with the alumni, I did feel I was
> effective as a representative and taken seriously. . . . I en-
> joyed the little bit of prestige that went along with being the
> President's daughter. I enjoyed the fascinating people I met;
> but I missed the camaraderie that other students had. I never
> had a conversation with anyone that didn't begin with, "Tell
> me what being the President's daughter is like?" And any
> male who asked me out on a date scored points for daring.
> . . . At Dartmouth I was silent. Except for theatre . . . that
> was wonderful. On stage I wasn't Jenny Kemeny . . .

From Rob:

> . . . I was automatically labeled as "the President's son"—for
> better or worse. . . . People assumed that because I was in a
> position to get information, I would always have it—imme-
> diately. If the College happened to put in a new toilet in one
> of the dormitories, I would be asked, "Why?" If I did not have a

concrete answer, there were always those who thought I was covering up. I was warned by the Admissions Director before I entered that I would face an unknown sort of prejudice. But I was confident that by being myself, I could survive. That by being a nice guy, people would look at me as just that. It was rough—some people resented me even for trying.

Going to Dartmouth, the children had one great advantage— the availability of our refrigerator. No matter how much they ate at Thayer dining hall, no matter how much they stuffed into their pockets, by 1 AM they were ravenous. One block away was sustenance. And they brought their friends. For a period I couldn't come into the kitchen late at night without falling over masses of students eating everything. Cinnamon toast was a favorite, but so was almost anything edible.

Too many mornings I was out of eggs, bread, milk, butter— and the leftovers I was planning to use for dinner. I began to write notes: "Don't touch." This did not work. I added, "Don't touch—or I will bite!" and finally "Poison!"

Once our son snuck in eighty-five people, and they cooked bacon and cinnamon toast, spaghetti and Hungarian goulash— much of which, unfortunately, ended up on the curtains or the ceiling!

Usually the students cleaned up reasonably well and eventually began to provide their own food. As long as I had prior notice, so I wouldn't appear in the kitchen *déshabillé,* Rob and we both agreed it was another way to bring about contact between the Presidency and the students—gut-level communication?

Every so often, while the children were at Dartmouth, we asked them home to dinner—though I expect they preferred to eat at Thayer, since the helpings were larger and there were thirds and fourths. We talked incessantly—between bites, during bites. It was natural for the children to tell of their accomplishments and failures, and sometimes complain about the College. John listened patiently to the major things, but when the conversation veered to nitpicking, he said, "I have office hours *for students only* every Tuesday. Come in and tell me then."

Both children lived in dormitories during their years at Dartmouth, but by good luck or bad both drew dormitories one block away from the President's House. One evening John and I were having dinner in the kitchen. Suddenly our son burst in the back door, grabbed the salt shaker from the table and began to run out.

"Rob! Where are you going with our salt?"

"I've got to get back to the dorm before the corn stops popping!"

"Damn it! Pretend you're at Yale."

During the student protests, Jenny twitted her father. Although she was still in high school and Dartmouth had not yet admitted women, she fantasized: "Daddy, suppose I were a student at Dartmouth and some of us were mad at the administration. Suppose we marched on the President's House. And suppose I was so furious I picked up something and threw it— through my own bedroom window!"

Rob was adept at handling exuberant alumni on the phone who either wanted to tell John what a "great President" he was or tell him their plan to save the world. He also spent immense amounts of telephone time talking to, calming down and listening at length to unhappy, neurotic, older women who would call asking for John, talk to Rob instead and call again later refusing to speak to anyone *but* Rob.

Jenny was particularly good with unhappy parents whose children had been turned down for admission to Dartmouth. Sometimes crying, these parents would come to the front door of the House, and Jenny would comfort them.

The median age of new college presidents is falling rapidly (a question of stamina). Many are in their mid-thirties or early forties. And frequently this means there are children, young or adolescent. The time consumed raising a family is enormous— emotionally, physically and logistically. If you're plain Mr. and Mrs. Jones, it's difficult enough. If you're Congressman and Mrs. or President and Mrs., it is really rough. The kids are sick and your exhausted husband has to go on a long road trip. Do you stay at home and feel guilty, or do you go with your husband and worry about the children?

You're hosting an important dinner party, while upstairs there is an upset adolescent who needs to talk—lengthily. Which has priority? Do you go to the football game that your son desperately wants one of you to see, the horse show your daughter has practiced jumping for week after week or to the dinner in New York at which your husband is to receive a prestigious scientific award? The choices are painful.

I thank whatever Fate kept me home on one occasion. John left for a meeting in Washington. Soon after, Jenny developed a grinding abdominal pain which I knew was *not* appendicitis, since she no longer had an appendix. The students had just returned from vacation, and each time they return they bring back with them some interesting bacterial or viral mutation. So I thought she had intestinal flu. When, after two days, she couldn't keep a thing down, including water, and had lost six pounds, I finally phoned the doctor. He came quickly and immediately called an ambulance to take her the one block to the hospital. And there she nearly died on the operating table from a gangrenous strangulated intestine.

My children have great faith in me. When John was asked whether he would take an ambassadorship if it were offered after the Presidency, he was blunt: "No way!" Rob sighed, relieved. "Great! Now I don't have to worry. If there was any injustice over there, Mummy would foment a civil war in six months!"

In any minor emotional situation I vocalize loudly; in fact, I shriek. If I'm exuberant I do it, if I'm furious I do it and I always do it when I can't find something. My first reaction is to yell that "*Someone put it somewhere else!*" When I later find it where I left it, I am suitably embarrassed—for five minutes.

One Fall I was on the telephone and heard some exciting news. I shrieked. My poor son, who was upstairs, bolted down, face blanched and shaking with fear. When I told him the good news, he gasped, "Oh, my God! I thought Daddy had had a heart attack, or you were bleeding to death!" That Christmas I received a small package from him. Inside was a shiny silver whistle, and an attached note which read: "Dear Mummy, to save *me* from a heart attack, please use this whistle when you are very exuberant and scream *only* when you are in trouble. Love, Rob." The only problem is that now I shriek when I can't find the whistle.

Can a five-year-old girl from a small college town in New Hampshire find happiness riding her first subway in Boston? No—because "There weren't any moles there!"

Five years later, can that same child, together with her younger brother, lead their mother through the labyrinths of the Toyko subway? Yes—when their city-hating mother refused to go shopping in the Ginza without clinging to her two young guides, who had learned the *entire* subway system in three days.

I can trace some of their independence and spunk and kindness back to one simple fact—that I cannot function in the morning. I *did* try to get their breakfast before school. But even as very small children they kindly suggested that I go back to bed!

Those two children are now grown up, earning their own living, not in secure small towns, but in two of the largest cities in the world—New York and Los Angeles. They are responsible and compassionate adults. And they are coping well. All because they had to get their own breakfast!

We arrived in Hanover in 1954. Three weeks later we had Jenny. I was approximately the age of a Dartmouth senior. Today I am the mother of two Dartmouth alumni. An entire generation has passed.

Commencement is a brilliant flash of color, if the June skies are blue.
Photo by Nancy Wasserman

That blond angel hid a devil plotting to get rid of an intruder—a baby sister. —Photo from author's collection

Today I am the mother of two Dartmouth alumni. An entire generation has passed.—Photos by Nancy Wasserman and David Pierce Studio

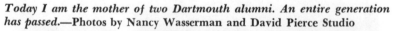

He still teaches two classes a year—usually one to freshmen.—Photo by Hathorn/Olson

Unlike most presidents, John writes every honorary degree citation himself. (With Ella Fitzgerald.)—Photo by Stuart Bratesman.

A receiving line can be a painful experience, a test of fortitude.—Photo by Adrian Bouchard

Judging the Winter Carnival Queen.—Photo by Adrian Bouchard

July's Summer Carnival is innocent fun. . . .
—Photo by Adrian Bouchard

My favorite is Bagel's baby, Cream Cheese.—Photo by John Kemeny

The Class of 1953, 684 men—and now one woman.—Photo by Nancy Wasserman

The year he came home scraped and bloody, I snapped that it was his last time at second base.—Photo by Nancy Wasserman

John explains that we will go on with the auction and that the protest has ten minutes.—Photo by Nancy Wasserman

Dartmouth bonfires . . . are a hexagon of railroad ties, tier upon tier, filled with combustibles. (Silhouette of John Kemeny.)—Photo by R. E. Nye

On Campus

IT WAS FOGGY and rainy, a nasty night outside, when two dozen members of the Students for a Democratic Society came to call. The SDS, vocal and vituperative in the late sixties, had calmed down several degrees by the Fall of 1970. They wanted only a minor confrontation with the President on the issue of Marine recruiting on campus. John moved out on the front steps to talk to them, for a discussion outdoors in the rain can shorten even the most vehement arguments. But everyone was so wet and bedraggled that I felt compassionate. "Come in and we'll go downstairs and have a fire."

We had lived in the President's House barely two months and hadn't yet used the basement room's enormous fireplace. Gratefully, the soggy students streamed downstairs and gathered in front of the fireplace where a fire was laid ready to light. Whoosh went the flames—lovely, cracking warmth. But the smoke, which was supposed to go up the chimney, didn't. It poured and poured into the room. The damper was jammed. The windows! Nailed shut as a foil for burglars. Amidst that blind group, coughing and crying and bumping into each other trying to find escape, I gasped my deathless line: "We're really *not* trying to tear gas you!"

That did it. Tension dissolved, and we continued the discussion upstairs. Nothing was resolved. But the students had seen the President, and the President had talked to the students. The next day the headline in *The Dartmouth* could have been:

"President Smokes Out SDS"—but they resisted the temptation.

Soon after, just before midnight, we heard a chant that increased to a roar. I turned off the lights in the upstairs bathroom, and peeked through the venetian blinds. Hundreds of students were marching down Webster Avenue, brandishing torches. They turned into our driveway and then sprinted for the front door which I thought would crack from the furious pounding. What were those torches for? Were they going to burn down the House? Courageously I opened the door and poked my nose out. With one voice they began: "1, 2, 3, 4 . . . 71, 72, 73, 74!" The mob was only a group of exuberant freshmen. This was their first week on campus, and the tide had turned.

With the lessening of student tensions, good-natured customs returned to campus. Students carol for us at Christmastime—sometimes from the back of an ancient fire engine. They make snowmen on the lawn, ring the bell and then scamper off. One undergraduate made a different snowman on the front steps five days in a row.

Spring on the calendar, but damn cold outside, 11 PM: At the door was a group of students dressed outlandishly and celebrating—what else but Mardi Gras—in the snow. This Spring visit is now an annual event. With a colorful, furled umbrella, they tap both shoulders, dubbing me something or other. My hand is kissed and I am crowned, then bedecked with gaudy necklaces. In my bathrobe, now bejeweled and bedazzled, I make a short thank-you speech. Then the ultimate award. My choice of a Tootsie Roll or bubble gum.

Halloween brings out the trick-or-treaters. Much thought is put into costumes. Some are ingenious. But a strict timetable is observed—college undergraduates are late-nighters. This means we stay up very late. The students leave the dinner hour for the neighborhood children and their accompanying parents. One Halloween we missed most of dinner, constantly leaping up to answer the bell and to put candy and UNICEF nickels into small outstretched paws. One group of children was particularly charming—five tiny figures dressed as ghosts. In the background the father waited patiently. I gushed over them, thrust lots of candy and nickels into their bags and was about to pat their heads, when those tiny ghosts grew and grew, *rising from their knees,* to at least six feet each. Their wispy tenor voices deepened to baritone as they serenaded me with "Men of Dartmouth." I had been conned—completely!

The Trustees were in town for their Fall meeting. With some other guests they were having cocktails, crowding the front hall of our House. There was a loud thumping on the front door. I opened it and was nearly trampled by the mass of rowdy students who burst in. A takeover of the President's House! "What else?" the guests thought, as they melted into other rooms. Fifty students *did* take over the hall, then chose a conductor and sang, a bit raucously: "Happy Birthday to you . . . Happy Birthday, Mrs. Kemeny. . . ."

"Streaking" made a brief but very vivid appearance on the Dartmouth campus in the early 1970's. The first publicized event took place in a crowded building when a group of male students, dressed *only* in ski masks, ran gleefully but rapidly through the corridors, astonishing the attendant. The following day her supervisor asked her, "Did you see those streakers in ski masks?" Stunned, the attendant replied, "You mean they wore ski masks?"

While almost everyone else on campus saw at least one streaker, I never caught a glimpse of one—even missing the young male who made a fleet foray through the entire House while I was in it. Just as I ran down the stairs and bellowed, he bolted out the back door.

Campus streaking soon became boring—nobody watched any more. Besides, it was too cold. Time for a new fad. Immediately another era was born, that of "The Pie in the Face—by Contract Only." No random hit or miss this, but a well-planned "hit" by "contract." Whipped cream, custard or meringue—the gooier, slurpier, squishier the better. The Big Green Mafia, as it was lovingly called, a shadowy syndicate of undergraduates, placed ads in *The Dartmouth* offering, for a price, to stalk, hit and splatter the victim. Several faculty members and a couple of deans were nabbed, and photographers, duly notified ahead of time, were there to record the event for posterity.

Would they get the President? They tried on the day he was dressed and ready to drive to Boston to speak to the alumni. If the pea-green Mafioso look-out hadn't been so careless, the ambush might have succeeded. But he kept zipping in and out of the lavatory across from the President's Office, arousing the suspicions of several secretaries. That lavatory's window had a perfect view of the waiting car below. Only through the gallant effort of John's Executive Assistant, Alex Fanelli, who thrust himself between the perpetrator bounding out of the bushes, pie up-raised, and the President, was John able to scoot into the car unscathed. I was hiding under the dashboard.

They would surely get John when it was announced that he would award prizes here at an Eastern NCAA swimming meet. I was so prepared for a splattered husband that I suggested he jump, fully clothed, into the pool and wash off the mess when it happened. A grand gesture, I explained. The Green Mafia missed their chance. He came home, dry and very pleased, to find the dessert I had cooked on the counter: lemon meringue pie.

Our license plates are in great demand. They have become collectors' items—mainly for us, since in a single year we lost or had ripped off *eight* separate plates.

Now these plates *do* have letters on them, words known to the entire community, not random numbers. LOGIC, one of John's professional specialties, and BASIC, the computer language he invented. I chose LOGIC, just in case I needed some. We had those license plates long before he took over the Presidency, and we plan to keep them after the Presidency. No coven of student collectors will coerce us into giving in and changing to numbers. It's the principle of the thing.

Besides the fact that replacing the plates is expensive, there is the time involved: Making out countless forms for the State of New Hampshire; waiting—sometimes a very long time—for the plates to return from the Concord State Prison; hand-lettering the cardboard, makeshift plates that have to be fastened on until the metal ones arrive; visiting the Chief of the Hanover Police for solace and advice; alerting the Campus Police to keep their eyes open—and cursing frequently.

I was mad enough to plot various nasty boobytraps. But when three plates disappeared in a single night, the Dean of the College issued an ultimatum to all fraternities: Return the plates *immediately* or be fined a hefty sum. Within four hours the three plates, and an apologetic note, appeared magically. Money talks!

The deep snows of Winter have almost gone; the temperature has risen above fifty, so we drag two chairs out to the patio and turn our faces to catch the pallid rays of a brief, Spring sun. Warmth, rebirth, peace. . . . Hell, no, The Rite of Spring is upon us! Eleven student windows are thrown open; eleven different stereos blast eleven different rock groups with eleven different beats. We flee inside (but not before our young male kitten runs wild with terror). The decibel level is as powerful as an earthquake, 9 on the Richter Scale. The pollution of the air spews across the Connecticut River to Norwich, Vermont, and angry residents call the Campus Police and the Hanover Police. One by one the windows close; one by one the amplifiers are turned off, until only one holdout remains, acidly raucous. But not for long. The roommate of the holdout sneaks into the room, changes the record and locks the door. From the last open window float the sweet and corny melodies of *The Wizard of Oz*. And the campus reacts. Bicyclists cycling, sunbathers sunning, the studious studying—all are caught in childhood nostalgia. And for a brief, brief period that afternoon a campus is humming and whistling and singing and smiling. A blissful Spring day.

Hanover dogs are notorious wanderers, and even the leash law doesn't faze them. They are still found rampaging through flower gardens, chasing Frisbees and softballs on the Green and cadging food in the dining hall. At Commencement, they loll in the aisles or sleep on the steps, blocking the seniors' way to the podium. Irish setters and black mongrels saunter on the platform, heedless of the hooded, black-robed elite, and the serious, formal occasion. For years dogs have interrupted every football game. A decade ago when John wrote a computer football program, I asked him to add an extra instruction which would randomly stop the game with the printout "dog on field."

In the Dartmouth stadium we are used to "times-out" for bounding dogs. ABC Sports was not. They were televising a football game which was being shown to most of the East. To television producers, seconds mean money—thousands of dollars. The inevitable dog appeared, seeming to know he was on camera. Instead of several short runs, he zig-zagged erratically, then stopped abruptly, putting his head down on his paws to wait—to wait until a sneaking pursuer was within two feet—and then off he romped again. Players and coaches and ball boys and policemen tried to catch him. And, each time the dog escaped, the crowd cheered. He was on national television, he was a star and he knew it. As a parting gesture to his fans he picked his spot and did what any normal dog would do on a grassy lawn—he went to the bathroom. And that afternoon the entire East Coast saw a fed-up referee smack down his flag on the mound—penalty!

So you're going to be in a motorcade. Not the ticker tape, Broadway variety, but still a real parade with balloons and bands and crowds. And a convertible for open-air viewing. The Governor will be just ahead, in a flashier convertible. Watch the Governor. He doesn't sit in the padded back seat. No, he climbs high up on the back. Imitate the Governor. There's no padding—just a maze of painful steel struts. The cars move; there's nothing to hang on to. Maintain dignity, wave tentatively, relax that fixed, embarrassed grin. Good Lord, look at the Governor! He's having an attack—body leaping up and down, head bobbing from side to side, arms in perpetual motion. Look again. It's not apoplexy; it's an attack of political euphoria. And it works. The crowd roars. Don't be outdone; imitate the Governor. Wave more lustily. Smile warmly at the little children. Make that person at the back of the crowd—the one with the glum expression—give in and grin. Forget inhibition and let it all hang out. Applause and cheers. You've won.

Bring a pillow and be a ham.

Coeducation had just begun. A blonde and bright Dartmouth woman—a sophomore—joined the women's crew. But it wasn't until she was in a shell, racing on the Charles River in Boston, that she truly felt a part of Dartmouth. On one of the bridges spanning the river stood a group of males—students and alumni —and they were shouting "Go Dartmouth Go!"—to her!

A Dartmouth Glee Club concert. During intermission a proud parent leaned over to me.

"Which one is yours?"

"All of them," I blithely replied.

I do talk ideas and hopes and minor problems with many students, but I am not their mother. That rare time when a serious problem arises, I send the student to a qualified person. We have a large pool of well-trained deans, guidance people and psychiatric counselors available. I've learned after practicing amateur psychiatry on my own two children *not* to tackle even one more—let alone four thousand!

One afternoon I was upstairs when loud thumpings began below. I cased the first floor. Nothing. The thumpings were coming from the basement area—louder and more frenetic. They were being made by a very inebriated freshman, vainly trying to open doors and finding that even turning knobs was impossible. He was an unusual sight, slim on top, but ballooning from the waist down. No doubt a lost lamb who had strayed from the flock at a nearby fraternity, where a very convivial costume party was in progress. But now he was in a strange basement, and he needed a bathroom—desperately! Quickly, I shoved him into one. Immediately there was a wail from inside. "I can't undo my pants!"

"O.K." I sighed, "Come out and I'll see what's the problem."

What a dilemma! His "costume" was composed of layers of waist-to-ankle flannel sweat pants—seven of them, one on top of another. And each pair had a narrow drawstring tied into several tight knots. No one, inebriated or sober, could have untied them all in time.

"Stay right there. I'll get the scissors!"

Soon a whimper from the bathroom. "I can't cut them, either!"

Seconds were precious now. I pulled him out, sawed away at seven tough drawstrings, shoved him back in and hoped.

Victory! He reappeared, contrite and very relieved. And then, like a mother with her toddler—and did he toddle—I took him by the hand. (His other hand was vainly trying to hold up seven pairs of slipping sweat pants.) I led him home and sternly told him not to stray again.

He reappeared at the door several days later, flushed, embarrassed and apologetic. I soothed him. A silly, amusing incident. Even drunk and very desperate, he had maintained dignity.

He has since graduated from Dartmouth with numerous honors.

It was early March, exams were imminent and the snow was sticky—three reasons to go on a rampage. Great roars echoed from the library area. Rob and I sneaked silently up behind the fraternities to come upon the greatest snowball battle the campus had ever seen. This was no helter-skelter bombardment. It was war, logistically and strategically. Each side had its generals, each side had its bullhorns, each side had its instructions.

"Right flank, forward!"

"Left flank, execute pincer movement!"

"Fire!"

Caught in that cross-fire, we found some parked cars and hid to avoid being massacred. I could scrunch down, but Rob, because of bad knees, was encased in thigh-to-ankle casts and walked like a robot. He could either lie flat in the snow or bend at the waist; he opted for the latter, his upper torso resting on the hood of a car. We were saved from destruction only by the arrival of a Campus Police car. Innocently they stopped, naively they parked and there they stayed. The battling forces united to pelt a more worthwhile victim, which rapidly became an ice-bunker.

Good naturedly, we accept student invitations to participate in various activities, sometimes silly, unexpected or undignified. Our rule is: Be a good sport, but don't become an undergraduate in the process. I have done everything from judging the Winter Carnival Queen to being a stand-up comic emcee at Spring Sing.

As a referee at crew races, John sat in the lead craft, hollering out directions and warnings to the crews racing behind him. "Too near New Hampshire! Too close to Vermont!" It was a fine afternoon. Not one boat went aground.

When John gets a frantic phone call at midnight from a fraternity, he rushes over. Who's dead? All the brothers are very much alive and ready to challenge him in the finals of a pinball tournament. He loses.

For several years John played second base for the administration in their annual baseball game against the students. The year he came home scraped and bloody, I snapped that it was his *last* time at second base. At 50, he would have to hang up his cleats. Groans from the students. But 20-year-olds have no idea what it's like to be half a century old with brittle bones!

Once I was an idiot, agreeing to ride a "bucking bronco." The "horse" was a battered, oil-drum contraption suspended by ropes and manipulated by two sturdy students. My objective was to climb up (which was very difficult) and to stay up (which was impossible). The students' only aim was to unseat the first lady, fast and hard. I got off my high horse in a hurry—upended in five seconds. Grass becomes concrete when hit rapidly from a height.

The center-of-the-Green statue for Winter Carnival one year was a massive St. Bernard lolling on a keg. The students underestimated the volume of snow that had to be sculpted, and they were way behind schedule. There was still much work to be done on the rear end, and only two days to go! That's when they called us, for publicity value. "Come out and work. See the President and his wife work." A photo session showed John chipping ice. It looked easy. It wasn't. Too gentle a swing and the ice-axe bounced toward his eyes. Too hard a chop and ice chips bounced towards his eyes. An announcer from WDCR, the student radio station, straddled the head of the dog, 30 feet in the air, offering commentary, rock music and free cocoa to the helpers. The kibitzers were many, the workers few, for the wind-chill factor that day was 25 below. (Two days hence, in all probability, the temperature would rise to 50 above. There is *always* a thaw for Carnival!)

The left leg, still mostly a frame of boards and chicken wire, definitely needed attention. Under the guidance of some undergraduates, we set to work packing it with slush made of snow mixed with icy water. We slapped on the slush, but it wouldn't stick. We pushed harder, but the wire bent and the slush dribbled through. Maybe the stuff would hold if we pushed *very* gently! I now had a proprietary interest in that left leg and berated the student next to me who had just knocked off my carefully constructed square foot of slush.

Cold, cold, cold! I kept slipping in the icy water. My leather gloves soaked through and my fingers were brittle. My ears had numbed and my nose dripped icicles. No Kleenex! I pictured a new sculpture on the Green: "Frozen First Lady."

None too soon, the grateful workers let us go. But we left with great admiration for those stalwarts, male and female, who had been there all day!

Back to the warmth of Parkhurst Hall. John strode into his outer office, coat dripping with melted slush, and announced gleefully, "Well, now they will *know* the President is all wet." The office staff pretended not to hear.

The student reporter was from *The Dartmouth*—shy and

young. Quickly, I prepared areas of discussion and mentally ran over a list of questions to feed him, priding myself at how expert I had become at twisting interviews my way. I needn't have bothered. He was way ahead of me.

That boyish face hid an agile mind; that innocent facade disarmed me. And when he went beyond the questions asked Mrs. Ford, I went beyond and answered them.

That evening, an unheard-of event occurred. Never has the editor of *The Dartmouth* called to check whether a story was accurate. (Never, because there are buttons on campus which have been worn by most faculty and administrators emblazoned with the statement, "I was misquoted by *The Dartmouth*.") But he called *me*. I reassured him. My answers? Of course I meant them. Then later: The interview was not that outrageous —or was it?

The article appeared the next morning, entitled "Candor on Tuck Drive." But something had happened, Thank God! There was little candor; it was restrained, innocuous. Had the students gotten cold feet?

No—they had just forgotten the layout man, an old Vermonter with strict ideas of propriety, who had decided to excise nine inches of copy. After several decades with the paper he has become the unofficial final arbiter. Now we all know where the ultimate decisions on editorial policy are made.

Conversations about the weather during Commencement weekend are not small talk. They are very serious, all-pervading discussions: Will we or won't we be able to hold a garden reception for three thousand seniors and parents in the President's garden? Will we or won't we attempt to have Commencement outdoors on the library lawn? (If we have to move the ceremonies inside to the arena, about four thousand people, mostly relatives, will have to be turned away.)

New England's weather is infamous—changeable, difficult to predict. And no two area weather bureaus can agree on the same forecast. Neither can the three local radio stations, all of which are within a radius of five miles. The White River station, just across the river in Vermont, gets its forecast from

Burlington, eighty miles to the northwest; the Hanover–Lebanon station uses the Concord weather bureau, sixty miles southeast; and Dartmouth Radio seems to rely solely on Minneapolis!

For the Friday night senior–parent reception in our garden, the final decision is mine. If I decide to go ahead outdoors instead of playing it safe (moving the whole thing upstairs in the arts center), the odds are that "possible scattered showers" will be sheets of heavy rain lasting most of the evening. And the torrent will sweep in just after the tables are set up with punch and cookies and the hordes of guests have descended.

If I miscalculate (i.e., trust a favorable forecast), then we will be drenched, the lawns chewed up, the punch diluted, the cookies crumbled and my House will be knee-deep in mud from the thousands whose invitation to the garden *also* includes a tour of the President's House.

One year I gambled and lost. The reception began at 8 PM; the heavens poured forth at 8:15 PM. But the mob came anyway. Hundreds and hundreds and hundreds of them. The lousy weather only seemed to make them more cheerful. We were all in the same boat (the *ark,* I think). Happy graduates, proud relatives, faithfully, patiently, stood in line—sometimes as much as half an hour—to greet us and shake our hands.

By 9:30 the line petered out; the garden was almost deserted. Cold, wet and completely miserable, we gratefully said goodbye to the last lingerers, then sloshed our way in, up the back stairs to the bedroom, peeling off wet clothes like contact paper. But soon—hot baths, steam heat!

Wailing, our married daughter (up from Manhattan with her husband to watch Rob graduate) burst into the bedroom. "There are thousands and thousands of people in the house! They haven't met you yet, and they're downstairs, *waiting!*"

Back on went the clothes, back downstairs we went. It was difficult. People were on the stairs; people were in every room on the first floor; they were in the coat closet; they were in the kitchen. Some had even settled on the counters. Wall-to-wall people, all with freshly cut wet grass and mud on their feet.

Still they came. (A definite lack of communication. I *had* told officials when we went in earlier that we were done, but somehow the message didn't reach the loud-speaker in the arts center, which blared all evening, "The President's House is open! The President's House is open!") Downstairs there was no semblance of a reception line; entrances were exits and vice versa. There was chaos. Squashed somewhere in the middle of a pulsating mass, we shook every hand we could see or feel, gulping air only when a moving body turned sideways to allow our chests to expand a few inches.

Sometime, very late, it was over—although people were still ringing the doorbell at 11. But by then all doors were *locked!* Collapsing on the hall stairs, we surveyed a ruin. Happily it was restorable. (Who would restore us?) Even a foot of mud on a cream Chinese rug *will* vacuum up if it is allowed to dry completely. Next year the downstairs will be wall-to-wall clear plastic; and, if I goof again, *we* will also be encased in it.

The annual question of where to hold Commencement is settled by John, the Dean and a committee of seniors. But that decision is made only after a small weather plane goes up about 8 AM to survey the skies. One Commencement morning, John called the Dean, "What does the weather plane predict?" "Nothing," replied the Dean. "Conditions were so lousy, it couldn't take off!"

Probability of rain was 99 percent, but the senior committee desperately wanted to take a chance, and the administration reluctantly agreed. It rained hard that morning—all around us, within two miles—but Hanover was spared. A professor, originally from Central Europe, thinks the term "Hohenzollern weather" should be changed to "Kemeny weather." It hasn't rained on one of John's Commencements—yet.

On the Road
(and in the Air)

IT WILL BE a repeat of yesterday and the day before that. Another city, another hotel, another bed. Another alumni tour.

Up early, a long, long day, then on to the next stop. Repack —neatly. Do not stuff! Check out, grab a taxi to the airport, check in and try to get the smoking section. Find the waiting area. Sit and wait. File onto the plane lemming-like. Sit and wait again. Miraculous! We are only fifteenth in line for takeoff. Die a little in the air, then land safely, breathe again and chalk up another successful survival test. Now hassle the baggage, queue up for a cab, get one and fervently wish we'd bypassed it. Inevitably the driver will be a frustrated jet pilot who has to prove he can outrace anything on the ground. Mechanized warfare with no ground rules. Oh, to be back in the air with a pilot who does *not* fantasize life as a cabbie!

Thoroughly shell-shocked, we make downtown, only to stand in line again to register. (Hope the room is ready; hope there *is* a room.) If all computers are working (i.e., human input is functioning), there may be.

The room's decor will be irrelevant, for it will be masked by mountains of baggage littering every bare space. What *is* relevant is that thing against the wall which we must ignore. If we so much as sit on it we'll flop down, fall asleep and forget to unpack the necessities for tomorrow. Perhaps that doesn't matter. The wrinkled look is in today—but will it be out by tomorrow?

Sleep comes in spite of air conditioning that spews out polluted hot dry air, in spite of the city's night noises, in spite of the clatter of the city's finest—its trash collectors. Don't curse the road crew operating the massive power drill at dawn, curse your husband. "John! You mis-set the alarm. It can't be morning already—it's still dark! (Or are the curtains closed?) Where's the light switch? Where's the bathroom? Where the hell are we?"

Groggy, we clean up and dress. Groping, we find our schedules. We do not speak. Dialogue before coffee is obscene.

Moving very slowly, we start out, perhaps meeting at odd times during the day. We will be together by evening for the reception, banquet and nightcap party.

John's day is a series of mad dashes from one event to another —an eighteen-hour marathon. That's what he's there for, to give his all, but he gives that and much more. Every minute is filled; if possible, overflowing. There is no time marked, "three deep breaths." For when the alumni club of X or Dartmouth's Alumni Office schedules a meeting of class agents at five o'clock at one end of the city and then a reception preceding the banquet across town at six o'clock, they don't allow time for transportation. I think they envision an immediately available cab, deserted streets and green lights all the way. No one seems to have heard of rush-hour traffic. A shower, a change before dinner, only occur in fantasies.

The usual places for the reception and banquet are hotel ballrooms, country clubs or motel convention centers. During his speeches, John must cope with the unexpected. He has had to endure a wedding reception (so exuberant it must have been Greek) in progress behind an unsoundproof partition. There was the time that Musak blared from two loudspeakers above him, drowning out every word. It took two electricians half the evening to disconnect the system. He has even had the radio calls of a distant taxi dispatcher interspersing his phrases over the microphone. And how many presidents have had to speak with a live and lively sea-cow cavorting right behind them?

My day will vary. If I'm not needed until evening, I grumble that I'm not being used enough, but if my day looks hectic I grumble about overuse. The usual routine will be a tour of the city, luncheon, shopping (if I have any money) or a chance to see an exhibit. I may sit in on a fund-raising meeting, have a scheduled interview—or an unscheduled one. I used to be the only woman at small select alumni luncheons. Now we ask wives: a more natural mix.

If there's time for a nap I grab it. I'm much more valuable after a nap, and nicer. John frequently has Q and A sessions with prospective students in the afternoon. I search out bright, interesting students who haven't yet made up their minds, and then I go to work selling the College; the beauty of the area, the specialness of the place, the emphasis on undergraduate education. Where else do you consistently find full professors teaching (and *wanting* to teach) freshmen? I will quote my husband, who has said that counting the number of Nobel laureates listed in an institution's catalogue is a useless exercise. Find out who teaches undergraduates. Occasionally now I will recognize a face on campus, dredge my memory and pull out that high-school senior I worked on a year or more ago in Cleveland or Seattle who *did* decide to come to Dartmouth.

I've been taken to the Cleveland Museum, Chicago's Art Institute and Contemporary Museum, the Taft Museum in Cincinnati, the "Sacred Circles" exhibit of Indian art in Kansas City, the San Diego Zoo and Carefree, Arizona. At NASA in Houston we had a private tour of Mission Control for the Apollo flights and met some very excited personnel who discussed the possibilities of a space-shuttle and a skylab—still on the drawing boards. (John was on parole and managed to see "Sacred Circles," the San Diego Zoo and NASA.)

The two of us join forces for the long evening. We are "on" —circulating, mingling and chattering. Cocktails (where are the canapés? I'm famished!), then the banquet, club business, speeches from club officers and the main event—John. Finally upstairs to a suite for a nightcap party. Encore tomorrow.

Often, the alumni club will make the day different and memorable. John has spoken at the Kennedy Center and in Alice

Tully Hall at Lincoln Center; the San Francisco alumni took over a large Chinese restaurant on Grant Street for an eight-course banquet. Los Angeles hired the Grand Dining Room of the Queen Mary, and alumni all over Los Angeles County were picked up in red double-decker London buses and transported to Long Beach.

One Spring the Washington, D.C., alumni club found an old menu (naturally covered in green plush) from the annual, then all-male, Dartmouth alumni dinner of the early nineteen hundreds. The meal was unbelievable—soups and seafood, wild game and roasts, vegetables smothered in cream sauces, condiments, savories and pastries. A different wine was poured with each course. It was a time of opulence—of food and girth. And the cost? Only $2.50. "Let's do the same menu for the Kemenys." I believe the lowest bid was from The Madison, which estimated a minimum of one hundred dollars—per person. We did *not* have that menu!

Yes, the circuit is exhausting, and it takes us a week to recover. But the trips are essential. We bring the College to the alumni, who want to hear from the top. We mend fences and make friends. We see new people, interesting people. We tour parts of the country, parts of the world we might never see otherwise. We absorb sights and cultures. And we can always add to our large collection of hair-raising tales—those insane rides with schizophrenic cabbies!

Beware of hotels whose enormous lobbies scream of opulence, plush and marble. These hotels were built when the comfort of the clientele came first. The bedrooms were spacious. The closets were walk-in. The bathrooms had bathtubs that could contain Wilt the Stilt comfortably. These hotels have kept their magnificent lobbies, but they have changed almost everything else—except their exorbitant prices.

Enter a bedroom now cut up to one-third its original size. It does have a picture window looking out on city lights or a beautiful bay. But the two of us can't pass the foot of the bed at the same time. (I'd rather look out at a brick wall in a room spacious enough to contain both of us *and* the furniture.) The closet is at least several inches deep. It sometimes has as many as four hangers. The rod was designed for miniskirts. The bathroom used to be the walk-in closet. But it is possible to turn around in the bathroom, because that marvelous old bathtub has been displaced by a new one—designed for a dwarf. In order to cover yourself partially with warm water (not hot—they have also done away with that *and* the steam I must have to hang out the wrinkles) clasp both arms tightly around hunched legs. This brings the water almost to your waist. By extending your legs toward the farther wall—which isn't very far—and keeping your upper torso upright, it is almost possible to cover your stomach with the luke-warm, rapidly cooling water.

If man's first priority is speed and cut-rate travel, he's got it with the airlines. If man's first priority is ugly conformity and the convenience of check-in, check-out automation, he's got it with the motels. But these priorities mean the demise of beauty and comfort and leisure in travel. Away with the great Atlantic liners—too expensive. Away with the Pullmans—too slow. Away with the grand hotels. How can ambience and service compare with cheapness and speed! If the Boston Ritz-Carlton ever succumbs to mediocrity, I shall give up travel permanently.

On our tours we are booked infrequently but tantalizingly into luxurious suites. These can be enjoyed at such times as the late evening after the impossible, exhausting, chock-full day—for those five minutes between undressing and collapsing on the bed. It is also possible to enjoy them for a full five minutes the next morning just before check-out time. Most exciting is catching a glimpse of an unused and heretofore unseen living room on the way out the door.

I like to eat well and regularly. I particularly need to eat late at night. But hotels and motels are not always ready to serve at 1 AM. Twenty-four-hour room service, serving *anything* edible, should be instituted for starving people like me. A growling stomach is not only uncomfortable; the noise also keeps me awake—to think about food.

But of course the world is geared to the conformist who gets up early, goes to bed by 10 PM and travels with his own refrigerator.

I have become a scavenger. I am omnivorous. I am a squirrel. I secrete caches of carrot curls, black olives and pieces of celery stolen from the dais and stuff them into my evening bag. Even stalks of celery, looking more like limp, bleached ropes of licorice, taste marvelous in the early hours. Croissants, butter and marmalade from breakfast trays are hidden in hotel drawers. To a desperate, famished person, hard, stale croissants can taste positively Parisian. Just before the room waiter wheels out our dinner cart, I have snatched lamb chop bones from our plates to be gnawed on later. And, in an emergency, I lap the sugar from the scant packet that cannot possibly contain a whole teaspoon!

Airplanes are fine places to collect: salted nuts, crackers in cellophane and small hunks of cheese wrapped in foil. But therein lies danger. When an awful odor wafts from the bedroom closet, do not search for sweaty sneakers. Instead, try rummaging through a pocketbook used on a trip two months earlier. No doubt you'll find a molding piece of Gruyère there.

Since we rarely stay in one city for more than a day or so, we have a problem. Bouncing from place to place necessitates foresight and expertise in packing. I ache to unpack at each spot; to put foldables in drawers and hang up crushables. But I can't. There's no time, so too often there is frantic pawing through my suitcases looking for the one item of clothing I packed too deeply. This messes up the system; it also musses up the clothes.

A still unsolvable problem arises in early Spring, when we go on a two-week trip from Hanover to Hawaii, with official stops in Boston, Los Angeles, San Francisco, Portland, Oregon, and Honolulu, ending with a few days of freedom on the Island of Hawaii. The weather is freezing in Hanover, cold and damp in Boston, 75 in Los Angeles, 55 in San Francisco, 65 in Portland and hot in the islands. I pack in layers. If the system works, the bottom layer of resort clothes are untouched (but very squashed) until Hawaii. But I can't predict any better than the weather bureau (whose record is abysmal) what the range of temperatures will be on the West Coast. What happens if our third stop, Los Angeles, has a heat wave? Out come the light-weight clothes from the bottom, and the entire system collapses.

Confronting pay-as-you-have-to-go public toilets while traveling has long been an affront to women. Thank God, New York and several other states have recently passed laws prohibiting this gross discrimination. But pay toilets do still exist. I haven't put money in a pay toilet for decades and won't ever. There are four alternatives: (1) Use the free stall if it is free (there are bus stations where they are so greedy they don't even have one of these). (2) Wait for a sympathetic woman to hold the door open. (3) Vault over (I used to do this; age has made it more difficult). (4) Crawl under (Here I am an expert, even in a long dress). The secret is to forget the stares, the ridiculous spectacle you may be making, and just reach your objective in time.

April is not the cruelest month. Take your pick: March or May, and sometimes part of June. In Hanover there is no gentle, languid Spring. We are teased with an 80-degree day on the last of March. Up pop the crocuses. Several days later we are pun-ished. Those green shoots are encased in an inch of ice or buried under two feet of snow. I remember the year that Buildings and Grounds had a removal job the day before Commencement. In the second week of June, trucks and crews were dispatched to the front of the gym to shovel up and dispose of two unsightly piles—piles of snow.

   We cannot grow magnolias or holly. It's usually too cold for dogwood; and often the apple blossoms are nipped by frost. The incredible changes in temperature—a 70-degree variation in one day—are too much for our emotional well-being. Grouchy after the long winter, we come out of hibernation, racked by cabin fever, only to be struck down by the newest virus brought back by the students returning from vacation. About this time I want to choke the idiots who still have "Think Snow" on their bumpers. By June, I want to kill them. The stickers are still on—not from neglect, procrastination or forgetfulness, but from a true desire to relive "eighteen hundred and froze to death."

Spring, when all our friends are winging south. Only stupid birds, and we, fly north. Alumni tour. The northern Midwest or northern New York State. It took us two years to realize that, while we were talking to alumni in Chicago or Buffalo, several vice presidents and other savvy administrators were doing the same in Fort Lauderdale or Phoenix.

"Presidents must have *some* prerogatives," I howled.

The following year we were in Atlanta, Miami and Houston at the right time. It is true that we are planning to do a nine-day stint of the Midwest this Spring. But I'm hopeful. It's scheduled for May.

Man has created a monster maze to bedevil his fellowman. More diabolical than any ever constructed for the rat, this maze with its obstacle courses and labyrinths reaching to infinity is known as the international airport.

The entrance is cluttered with many people anxious to grab your bags, tag them and send them to the appropriate airline. In their haste, however, they are as likely to send them to Chattanooga as Chicago. This hazard forces us to carry enough baggage onto the plane to tide us over until the lost baggage is returned. We frequently have to make three changes of clothing a day and don't have time to buy replacements. (If I had the time, I'd happily do it and bill the airline.) So I am stuck with a garment bag which has to be long enough to hold floor-length dresses. Even folded over, the damn thing drags on the ground, so my right arm must be extended straight out to carry it. The other hand holds a jam-packed and very heavy carry-on case— its dimensions supposedly conforming to airline regulations. (Beware: Airline dimensions vary and, after all that careful planning, it may be grabbed away and you'll spend the rest of the flight wondering if it will ever reappear.) With all those helpful porters at the entrance, it's no wonder there are none *anywhere* in the airport itself. I've heard of shopping carts; I've yet to see one. And I don't look quite infirm enough to commandeer a wheelchair. So off we limp, struggling to tote the luggage, the coats, the pocketbook—mine is large and full enough to use on safari. (We have a friend who says that even if she's off to London, she packs as though the next trading post were 4000 miles away.)

There must be a plot. Why is our gate always at the very end of the farthest concourse? Miles to go before I sit! And part way there one goes through that checkpoint where everything is opened. Now, I have carefully smushed everything into my bags and then jumped on them to close and zip them. The nice lady who uncloses and unzips doesn't do that. Consequently, she has trouble reclosing them. She pulls and tugs and glares at me— and finally rips the zipper. Two broken zippers so far. And we still have a way to go, with slips and shoes now popping out from all sides. We switch bags to vary the weight on our arms. (Later I will realize that the flu symptoms I get on every alumni trip—aches in my neck and back and arms—are not psychosomatic, but excruciating lameness.) We *will* reach the gate and we *will* fly and we will probably land. And then, with luck, we may claim our other luggage at the carousel. But that will take time, because there is a law which states that for every three pieces of luggage, two will slide down together almost immediately, while the third will appear only after all the other passengers have long since disappeared.

In 1969 my husband announced that he was giving up flying forever. In 1970 he became President of Dartmouth, and off we flew again—thousands and thousands of miles for Dartmouth. We do not enjoy it.

I worry constantly about all the things that can go wrong; John suffers from severe motion sickness. If there's turbulence and the plane drops a hundred feet, I know that we will crash. My sick husband hopes we will.

I do realize that our time is at a premium, and the only way to tour the country rapidly on our alumni trips is by air. It's just that I never forget I'm in an airplane. Prior to takeoff I carefully check the weather forecast for the terrible threes— turbulence, thunderstorms and tornados. I case the waiting area for a potential hijacker, using everything I can remember about that psychological profile. And at the moment of takeoff I keep an eagle eye out for any flocks of birds on the runway grouping to clog up the engines. Gripping the armrests with whitening knuckles as we ascend is not unusual, nor is my mental and physical torment until the No Smoking sign flashes off. Why is it that I am always the last to receive my cocktail, when I need it *immediately?* I quickly learn where the lifebelt is kept and whether my seat cushion is a flotation pillow. I always keep my seat back in an upright position and never unfasten my seat belt except to go to the lavatory. When the plane drops suddenly, *I* will not be the one to crash into the ceiling, nor will I follow a suddenly sucked-out window as some unfortunate and untethered stewardesses have.

My repertoire includes such interesting facts as the minimum height of clearance for the seawall in Boston and the correct angle of descent into San Diego. I rate water approaches from Hong Kong to Harrisburg according to degree of difficulty. I know which airline has the lowest rate of fatalities and which airport has the highest rate of accidents. I am truly delighted that most air travel is by jet now, for at least I don't have to monitor the wing motors for possible fires. I have learned that most of those awful bumpings over cities are the result of heat inversion and will be over soon—if we land soon. Stacked up, circling and bouncing for several hours is unpleasant, particularly when you lose confidence in the accuracy of the fuel tank gauges. Those grindings and thumps as we prepare to land *should* mean that the landing gear is being lowered—not that the aircraft has metal fatigue and is falling apart. But even if the aircraft holds together, suppose the air traffic controller suffers from mental fatigue and falls apart? If your plane has clearance to land and then, within five feet of the ground, swoops up suddenly, the pilot is not giving the passengers an added thrill. He is skillfully trying to avoid smashing into a corporate jet *also* with clearance to land—on the same runway. (No wonder the greatest probability of crashing occurs on landing.) If we do reach the ground, that scream of the engines and the crushing force of several G's should mean that we are coming to a stop, not that the brakes have failed. If Ray Bradbury, that acclaimed writer of science fiction and proponent of space travel, can call himself a "practising coward" and refuse to fly, I don't know why I can't wistfully hope that sometime, somehow, we will cut out a couple of stops and alumni-hop leisurely—by train.

My husband has a habit which I am convinced he does only to annoy. He cannot sneeze once or twice discreetly. He throws himself into his sneeze and explodes seven or eight times in a row. The noise and reverberation are terrifying—reminiscent of a bazooka. More than once a concerned stewardess has rushed to his side ready to give resuscitation. He is not suitably embarrassed.

The end of another alumni tour. A coast-to-coast flight—Los Angeles to Boston. We scrutinized the passengers as usual, warily on the lookout for one who might fit the hijacker profile. And we found one. He was scruffy and long-haired (but then most nice students are). However, his eyes darted about, and he favored his right arm, where there was a small but noticeable bulge which he was trying to conceal. Should we have reported it? Should we have caused a fuss? We did neither and worried all the way across the country. But there was no hijacking; we landed safely. And the young man? He was in the Boston baggage-claim area. His eyes were not darting fearfully anymore; in fact he was grinning broadly. The bulge was no longer under his sleeve—in his hand was a tiny, well-traveled, coal-black kitten.

On Stage

As the President's wife, I have traveled at least 100,000 miles for Dartmouth (mostly by air); visited eighty-odd cities in twenty-four states and two foreign countries; attended more than a thousand outside functions; prepared and hostessed at least six hundred events at the President's House; turned down something like twenty-five hundred invitations; spoken to and shaken the hands of several hundred thousand people. (I do not count the hands reshaken!)

From the start I found a few men *and* women who assumed that my thoughts were carbon copies of John's; who heard my words as his; and who saw my actions only as manipulations by that Great Puppeteer—the President. They gave me no credit for having an independent brain.

There was no problem at first. Newspapers, eager for interviews from a new, fairly young first lady, asked only frothy questions suitable for the society pages. "What is the color scheme of your living room? What famous people have you entertained? Who are your favorite dress designers? (Ha!) What are your favorite dishes and how many are coming to dinner?" Innocuous stuff. No thinking involved.

In the second year the questions became more meaty. Interviews began to show up in the Living sections rather than on the society pages. No one had ever implied that I shouldn't speak out. But could I answer questions honestly from my own point of view and not be accused of speaking for John? Could

I be accurate on sensitive subjects? How much did I know, anyway?

Los Angeles: The reporter from the *Los Angeles Times* was a woman, as all my other interviewers had been. I was ready for another gentle probing of my decorating style and cooking secrets. But she was different—very bright and very sharp. She did not want answers from a hostess; she wanted answers from one half of a team. I wasn't prepared for her line of questioning. I wasn't even prepared for an interview, for arrangements were made on twenty minutes' notice.

We sat on a park bench in Pershing Square, watched by winos and other reclining types. In eight hours I had moved from Winter in Hanover to Spring in California. The sun was warm, I began to relax and I talked my head off. The reporter's questions were good and tougher than any I had met before—about the College and education in general. Frantically, I tried to pull facts and numbers from my subconscious, praying my answers were remotely on target.

Racing back to the hotel I panicked, picturing a million readers reading *my* interview. What had I said? I couldn't remember. I knew I had spouted. How much of that flow was wrong? How much was garbage? Maybe it wouldn't be printed. But it was—and near the News section! Forty-two column inches (I measured). The article read well, was accurate—even a bit witty—and it *sounded* like me. But the accompanying picture did *not* look like me.

No interview could ever frighten me as much again. So I could take with more equanimity the next "unscheduled" one two days later. On the way in from the San Francisco airport, I was informed by an alumnus that an interview was set up for me with the *Examiner* "as soon as you check into the hotel." There was one problem. Our room wasn't ready, but the reporter and photographer were. In a borrowed hotel room, grimy, tired and still in traveling clothes, I had another session of grilling, with more confidence and a very sympathetic photographer. Reading the interview the next day, I was immensely impressed with myself and eternally grateful to the photographer, who had not only erased all the grime, but had obliterated the circles under my eyes.

I've now been questioned from Boston to the West Coast; from Cincinnati to Atlanta. I still get some frothy questions, but most tend to be hard and more interesting: "What is this year's operating College budget, and how much goes for faculty salaries? How much financial support does the College receive from the federal government? What are the College's criteria for financial aid? Discuss student attitudes on sex, drugs. How much apathy do you see on the part of the students? Compare it to five years ago—ten years ago. What are the issues on campus this year? Discuss affirmative action, and how does Dartmouth stand with HEW? What are the problems of minority groups on campus? Is there discrimination? Reverse discrimination? Will you comment on national politics? Describe the Dartmouth Plan—its strengths and weaknesses. What is the Ivy League policy on athletic scholarships? What percentage of your students go on to graduate school? What is the College's investment policy vis-à-vis South Africa?"

John can answer these better than I and in much more detail, but he's not there. The questions are directed at me.

I am not a constant scholar. I bone up periodically. A lot can be learned from reading; more from listening and soaking up information by osmosis. I try to differentiate rot from truth, fable from fact. I am learning not to generalize, to give simplistic answers or use bad analogies. I don't always succeed. I'm better now at ad-libs, at knowing when to stop answering and how to feed questions I want to answer. And, most importantly, I can admit, "I don't know."

My media appearances (not including newspaper interviews) have been spotty—mostly limited to local radio and TV.

I have appeared on Boston television's *Good Morning Show,* when they grabbed me at the last minute. There I was in my scruffiest jacket, no lipstick, my hair a tangled mess. Even so, I think I ad-libbed rather well.

When John and I were scheduled to do a TV talk show in

San Francisco, there was a slight complication. Just as we arrived, out went all the municipal workers on strike, the cameras with them.

And there was the time I was supposed to be interviewed on Chicago television. I wasn't (pre-empted by Woody Allen). He's wittier—I'm prettier.

Interviews are one thing; a formal speech is quite another. Audiences don't faze me; nor do I worry about a dearth of material. I can organize and write a good speech; but then I have to read it, losing verve and spontaneity—and probably my place in the text. I can memorize the speech, but that seems cowardly and theatrical. Instead, I jot down a series of notes, key words, on the topics I want to cover, with an approximate time limit written beside each. Every topic should have an ending with a natural lead-in to the following one. When *used,* this method works. It takes only one quick glance down at those brief notes and at your watch to trigger a response: "Get off the present subject, and proceed to the next one. Do not pass Go!" But inevitably I do. There is no guiding genie to jostle me, to scream in my ear, "Look down at your notes, dimwit!"

If one of the topics involves me emotionally, I attack it spiritedly. I touch on every ramification, however remote. I digress further and further, moving from one obscure tangent to a more obscure tangent of that tangent. When that line peters out, I am left dangling helplessly over an abyss of silence —my own.

Nothing to say. No place to go. I can't leap back gracefully to a new topic; I can't even inch my way back—the route I charted is much too complicated. Trapped, I remember the watch. Maybe there's time to salvage something. Disaster—way over the allotted time. Ad-lib an ending, quickly. A few, feeble fumblings and my organized speech is over. A bust. No one will ever hear the final two topics, and they will miss forever my superlative summing-up and climactic conclusion.

I came to this job with one very valuable attribute—an ability to carry on a conversation on almost any subject with almost anyone. I'm a master of surface conversation; I can go deeper if the situation requires, at least on some topics.

People interest me; all people, even ones I dislike or loathe. No matter how boring, garrulous, crude, egotistical, Neanderthal, mousy or maniacally radical the type, somewhere each has one redeeming feature—an interest that we can both latch on to. The trick is to find that something. I possess an avid curiosity and immense store of trivia. By probing, digging deep into my mine of information, I can uncover some nugget that brings a gleam into my partner's eye, and from there it's easy.

I have to carry on conversations with thousands of diverse types, talk and make sense. I enjoy this part of the job, for it's almost a game. What does he or she really care about that is not related to his or her job or public accomplishment? First, flatter the ego and ask a few questions about the public person. Listen, really listen, and then go to the less obvious.

Try an actor on honesty in government; a foundation head on sculpture; a university president on mountain climbing; a composer on horse racing; a vice president on oriental art versus abstract art; a symphony conductor on the problems of Northern Ireland. Discuss beautiful women with a Nobel laureate; with an Earl, discuss a common problem—our children's bad spelling; or discover that a Dartmouth Trustee is an expert on Heath Kits and CB radios. I have never been coy and rarely a hypocrite who dances around the issues. Candor and bluntness come easily. I was a superb fund-raiser in several local drives for just these reasons: If you believe the product is good, *sell it;* if your prospective donor has the means to fund it, *tell him* to buy in; don't minuet.

I argue politics, national problems and Dartmouth decisions with the Trustees and alumni. The debates are real and stimulating—sometimes heated, but not nasty. I don't play around with meaningless, socially acceptable neutrality.

When all else fails, I try humor. However, even that failed me twice, with a few Weatherpeople and some frenetic feminists. Levity is *not* a part of their manifestos.

The human brain is a wondrous thing—a giant computer. And a well-functioning memory bank to which there is easy access and instant retrieval is an invaluable asset. In this job a memory for names and faces is essential, particularly if your husband has a lousy one. For years mine functioned flawlessly. I could absorb masses of information about great numbers of people—names, faces and interesting tidbits—and then retrieve when necessary. Finding the relevant data, sorting it and instantly identifying an individual from all the thousands of others, was a breeze.

I could meet Mr. Jones once. Years later I would recognize him again, even in Thailand, and also be able to dredge up other bits—that his daughter went to Stanford Business School, was now an investment banker and painted abstracts.

Not anymore. Recently I have begun to malfunction occasionally, either from overuse or an overload, or both. An overused memory can grow old, wear out, rust; and its storage bank will bulge beyond capacity if the flow of data to be absorbed is continuous. In my case the flow never stops, the people keep coming. And a tired brain complains with a short circuit. Take a Chicago alumnus I meet for the first time. I still may be able to absorb some pertinent facts about him, but when my memory logs all the data, he has been irrevocably placed and categorized under the heading *Chicago*. Placed in Chicago, he belongs there and there only. He certainly does *not* belong in my garden! He does not compute in Hanover, therefore we have never met.

Once I even had the talent to recognize that rare type who saunters up with the greeting, "Bet you can't guess who I am?" Today I snap back, "You are so right!"

To prove how far I've slipped, a recent example verbatim:
"Hello. I'm Jean Kemeny."
"I know. We had a lengthy conversation a week ago."

Being well briefed about people, their habits, their idiosyncrasies is a necessary, vital part of the job. Briefings will arrive in massive quantities from administrative offices for our use on tours, at receptions—for any gathering. I am always very well briefed the *second time* when someone forgot to include important data the *first time;* and I have a mass of my own information gathered over the years.

Before any trip, before any function, I read an immense folder containing general information and capsule profiles of the interesting and/or important people I'm likely to meet, or even remotely likely to meet. There have been gaps in this data.

On a trip to Washington, D.C., several of us were invited early one morning to meet Mrs. William Rogers, the wife of the then-Secretary of State. She planned to greet us in a magnificent room atop the State Department, and we would have a private tour. Mrs. Rogers was most kind and must have had extraordinary staying powers; she had been up until the early hours in that room hostessing the annual black-tie affair for the entire Diplomatic Corps, *and* as soon as she left us she would teach grade school!

At the last possible minute, a brown paper bag was shoved into my hands by some young Dartmouth administrator. "Present this to Mrs. Rogers on behalf of Dartmouth." Inside the bag was a book *The College on the Hill,* a good modern history of the College. Quickly I prepared a few remarks in the elevator, delivered them haltingly to Mrs. Rogers, who then graciously accepted my gift—a brown bag! I had forgotten to take the book out. And then the real slip-up in the briefing. Mrs. Rogers thanked me and Dartmouth and then said, "I recognize you from your pictures, Mrs. Kemeny."

No one had briefed her that well. And certainly the State Department does not have pictures of college president's wives —at least I hope they don't. (During *that* administration there may have been dossiers on anyone who ever opened his mouth.) I stuttered and gulped and muttered something. And as soon as I could get away, I grabbed someone from Dartmouth and howled, "How did she know what I looked like? Where has she seen me before?"

He treated me like an idiot child. "In the *Dartmouth Alumni Magazine.* As a parent she receives it every month. You know, of course, that their son graduated in the late 1960's."

I do now!

I also must know the internal news—town and gown. That which is for publication and that which is not. It is assumed that I am the first to know the latter. False! I am usually the last to know. This lack frequently gets me into trouble. I beg for updates (my husband, as shown elsewhere, is hopeless). I designate someone as my official "updater." This person performs well, feeding me undercover news, for a few months. Then the vigilance relaxes, peters out. My desperate need is forgotten. And I am left with my foot in my mouth—again.

At a reception: "Hi, ———. Didn't you bring your wife?"

"We've been separated for six months. Didn't *you* know?" (No!)

On the telephone: "Can you and your husband come to cocktails next week?"

Long pause. "We can't come! He's—run off with another woman!"

At a clothing store: A young administrator is looking at expensive three-piece suits. He asks my opinion, "Which ones shall I take?"

Airily, wittily. "You mean 'which one.' Dartmouth certainly doesn't pay you enough for all of these!"

Strange look, weak laugh from young man.

I bring up the incident to John that evening as an example of my amusing repartee. Most amusing. No one thought to tell me that the young administrator had already resigned several weeks earlier to take a lucrative position in Manhattan.

At times I am moved to find jobs for seniors or recent graduates. This involves writing letters to contacts in advertising, films, industry or journalism. Usually there is no opening, or just a crack, but I keep trying the doors.

Another method is face-to-face confrontation. After the student tells me what he or she is interested in, I scan the room for an alumnus with the same interest who might be hiring. By maneuvering, I pull them together, do some introductions to break the ice and then tell the alumnus not to miss a good prospect.

There was one student and one alumnus I practically dragged towards each other. The young man was slightly embarrassed; the alumnus seemed put out, bored. Another failure. Maybe I was too blunt? Two years later I saw the young man again. He was working in film; for two years he had had a good job—with that alumnus! One success.

The seating arrangement at almost every banquet includes a head table resting on a dais. I have sat at such somewhere between one and two hundred times. The possible number appalls me, so I have ceased counting.

Before being seated I invariably check two items: The length of the tablecloth: Is it long enough in front to cover feet behind? The dais: Do the wooden supports have any uneven boards?

There is only one advantage in being seated high above the throng. Being "honored guests," you are served first.

The disadvantages of being up there facing the crowd are numerous. If you eat first, every bite is monitored by the hungry group below. In fact, every lapse, every goof, is monitored the entire evening.

Long, bell-shaped sleeves should not be worn. I cannot converse and hold my hands still; in fact, if I had no arms, I could not speak. Any sweeping gesture to emphasize a point will include a sweeping sleeve—upending a wine glass or picking up morsels of food to distribute them indiscriminately. Perhaps long sleeves should not be worn at all. Once I discovered a rapidly melting glob of orange sherbet on the elbow of a cream-colored dress. Dabbing at it only enlarged the bright orange area. Quick thinking saved the dress and delighted the Goops. (For the uneducated, *The Goops* is a classic tale of manners for children, about nasty little things who had no manners.) I plunged my entire elbow in my water glass and diluted the sherbet.

The length of the tablecloth is very important. It must reach below the table to hide the fact that I have taken off my shoes. I do not take off my shoes if: (1) There is only a short space between me and the edge of the dais, for then there is a real and present danger that one or both shoes will drop off and be unreachable. (2) It has been a long day. Once my feet are liberated from shoes they will swell and swell, and there will be no way to squeeze them back in.

After dinner and conversation there are the speeches. Sometimes there are several of them. The response will be either polite applause or a standing ovation. Standing ovations are more numerous than one would imagine, and preparations must be made to rise in a split second. Such preparations should include: (1) Placing your napkin on the table. If it is kept in your lap, either it will fall to the floor when you rise, or, if you grab it to prevent its falling, you will end up clapping a napkin, not your hands. (2) Make sure your shoes are on. Groping to find them is most awkward, particularly when one has disappeared. (3) Beware of crossing your legs under the table. This can be dangerous. Frequently one leg will go to sleep, and leaning on the table to keep your balance makes applauding impossible. (4) If the planking is uneven, it will be *your* chair whose leg will be caught in the gap as you abruptly push it out to stand. This will involve frantic maneuvers to keep from sliding off the tilted seat, and, at the same time, desperate tuggings to lift the bloody chair leg from the vise that holds it.

Success! The chair moves backwards ever so smoothly. Graciously you rise, applauding—quite alone.

Our ancestors may have thrown out King George, but two hundred years later we fawn, star-struck, over his several times great-granddaughter. Our Imperial Presidency has gone—disgraced. "Hail to the Chief" has been displaced. Still, there is glamour in all the glitter of visiting royalty—a sneaking envy for all that pomp and circumstance.

After being addressed on numerous occasions as "The First Lady of Dartmouth" in this country and "Madame President" abroad, an insidious change occurred. I began to pretend I was just a bit royal. Having bills come addressed to "The Palace" from downtown merchants was fun. Nodding from a balcony to throngs below; circling my hand lazily to crowds lining the routes of motorcades; having lunch in the White House or dining elegantly in London's Goldsmiths' Hall to the pounding chant of "M'Lords, Ladies and Gentlemen" was intoxicating. But the fillip which pushed me over the edge into fantasy was the deep, royal curtsey given to me by a former British Music Hall star, her voice still superb, who had once given a similar curtsey during the war at a command performance for the King of England. I succumbed to feeling queenly. I reveled in it—a most undemocratic and elitist feeling, but quite delicious.

Hubris. But the gods will have their revenge! My overinflated balloon was pricked and with a tired, sad pop I was brought back to earth—hard—by the menial chores I do that no queen *ever* thought of doing. I am a President's wife with only part-time help, who has to cope alone at times. Would a queen sit in a fumey, greasy garage for three hours on a blistering hot day? Would she patiently sit there and perspire, waiting for a mechanic to patch up the salt-eaten, rusted undercarriage on a Jeep so it could pass inspection for a few more months? Would she carry in heavy groceries in flimsy bags which always seem to split open just as the concrete back steps are reached? Would a queen tiptoe barefoot downstairs for a midnight snack? No. She would ring. But, if, as a lark, she did try it, would she invariably step into a very warm puddle made by a careless, lazy cat? I now wear slippers in the evening. And the dog—she always times her up-chucks on rugs or chairs after the help has left, but only *minutes before* the arrival of unexpected visitors. I clean up the messes. Life in the palace was never like this.

Backstage

THERE ARE some things it is better not to know ahead of time. For example: the amount of documentation and planning ahead implicit in and necessary for my job.

For several decades I survived doing as little of either as possible. Thinking ahead meant curbing impulsive action. It meant organizing thoughts; boring, unnecessary work. That sign "Plan Ahea$_d$" didn't fit me. My sign would have had room only for a magnificent "P," with all the other letters squashed in. IBM would have disowned me, stripping me of its plaque "THINK" as ignominiously as the military tears the rank from a dishonored soldier.

I detested documenting anything. I forgot to write thank-you notes, ignored letters to friends and relatives and never made lists of things to do. Occasionally I did make out grocery lists, but by the time I reached the store, my list was always lost. Although I bought a new filing cabinet, any attempt to find a relevant clipping failed—usually because the entire folder was missing.

With a guilty twinge, I look at a platter we received nearly thirty years ago as a wedding present; the thank-you note still hasn't been written. And it took a desperate cable from my future husband in Europe, read movingly to me over the phone by the local telephone operator, to goad me into answering his letters more often. He had written faithfully; I hadn't.

As a freshman at Smith, I may have sent as many as two letters home during the first six months. My mother wrote me each week—amusing, newsy letters. But sometime in February she fixed me. Another fat letter arrived. I tore it open, to find ten pages totally blank. Or almost blank. On the last page were two words—"You rat!"

My comeuppance had to come. I am serving penance for more years than I want to count, organizing and documenting. Years at hard labor which are a matter of survival.

Each quarter I must list the number of guests entertained; the type (student, faculty, foundation officer, visitor, etc.); the kind of event (breakfast, supper, dinner, luncheon, cocktails); the cost of extra help for large functions; the amount of liquor bought; and plants, bulbs, candles, mop pails, a new lamp—any item purchased for the President's House. All receipts and invoices must be saved and attached, otherwise we are not reimbursed.

Periodically I send in written evaluations of the staff and administrators with whom I work. Every two weeks I make out staff sheets detailing hours worked, vacation, sick leave and personal days taken. These sheets must be delivered to the Payroll Office on time, or the staff is not paid.

I keep a personal card file of every event I have ever given— when, who came and what they ate and drank.

For the first two years I made out a card (with picture, if possible) on every member of the faculty, administration, staff, professors emeriti, widows and widowers connected with the College. Each card had name, rank, spouse's name, undergraduate school and any other pertinent information. The idea was much too complicated; trying to keep it current was impossible.

I keep no diary. But I do tack a calendar of upcoming events for the month on the bulletin board. I have begun to tack up two months at a time, having once forgotten an event on the first of the following month. (See "People, Parties and Patter.")

I have no social secretary and must rely on John's office for very large jobs, such as addressing 2000 invitations or culling names for Commencement Luncheon, and for hundreds of smaller jobs when I am frantic, which is often.

Now I write notes and letters—thousands of them—thank-yous, sympathy, congratulatory. My record is far from perfect, but I *am* much better.

Lists. I live with lists. I cannot live *without* lists. I even make lists of lists. There are scribbled notes to myself scattered over the entire House—under the bed, under piles of books, on kitchen counters, behind the bed, in drawers, under the radiator, in the bed. . . . Many of these are out of date by the time they are rediscovered.

I have a list of every piece of art borrowed from the College; I also keep a record of every gift to the President's House, and I have to be able to lay my hands on any piece at a moment's notice. And then there is a periodic inventory of the entire House for purposes of re-evaluation and insurance. This requires a day of traipsing through four floors, muttering—"That's yours, that's mine." For this effort, at least, I receive a computer printout!

Our daughter, Jenny, was to be married in Hanover, but since she was working in New York, I kept a *precise* list of every wedding present, with description and name and address of the sender. She would not be allowed to follow in my forgetful footsteps. I was so organized for that wedding, that I drove everyone bats. My filing system was meticulous, putting bills and letters in the trash and envelopes in the refrigerator.

Then there are the nightly epistles to the staff. Doesn't everyone do that in bed?

I am used to compliments about the President's House. The kitchen—"so well designed and *so* convenient"; the living room —"such lovely colors"; the plant room—"spectacular!" (The latter is a greenhouse-like room with a southern exposure off the living room.)

Abloom and fragrant most of the year with Christmas cacti, African violets, daffodils, tulips, hyacinths and orchids, the plant room draws gasps from visitors. I smile humbly. I can take some credit for the glass-topped tables and white iron chairs (we hold many dinner parties here) and for the plan to lower the ceiling and install better lighting. Unhappily, I must confess that I can take absolutely *no* credit for the growing things. I do buy new tubers, seeds and bulbs; I choose the colors and write the checks. That's all. Doug McBain, houseman and gardener extraordinaire, does all the rest. I do not plant, water, feed, repot, prune or talk to the things. I don't dare. I was born with a love of gardening, but a black thumb. It's probably a lack of patience; I want to see results immediately.

Once I did use patience on radishes. The most incompetent gardener can grow radishes. How plump and red they looked in the catalogue. I followed all the directions on the seed packet. I readied the soil; I planted the seeds and gave them sun and food and water. Result? They weren't round. They weren't red. Were they possibly a new strain—pale pink parsnips?

In the beginning were the Words—*expense account.* Like one who finds sunken treasure, I suddenly had at my disposal an immense sum, seemingly infinite, but renewable yearly. The "Account for House and Representation" was its official title, and from it came funds to cover the expenses for the House (recovering a chair, replacing a rug, cleaning the curtains). The H and R account would always be there when I needed it—a bottomless well of money.

New to the job, new to massive entertaining, but now blasé about costs, I found myself having to manage a large house, direct half-a-dozen staff and entertain on a large scale. Not to the manor born, I felt required to act as though I had been.

But how could I direct the staff to organize a dinner for thirty when I had no idea where to begin? The answer was simple—I wouldn't have to direct. I would use my life preserver, the expense account. With that cushion, I could call the caterer, order dinner for any number and relax. Let others worry and work. I would be fresh and unharried. One phone call and the food appeared magically—delicious dinners for three dozen, cocktail hors d'oeuvres for one hundred, exquisite late evening suppers for a few. What a spree I had, securely enveloped in liquid assets; what a blithe spirit I was, entertaining lavishly, totally ignoring small details like costs.

Those small details: I never asked for an estimate of anything. I forgot that tenderloin tips and frosted grapes weren't
free, nor was labor. I didn't know that the caterers were notorious for late billings—but those bills *would* arrive.

Six months later they came, a deluge of them for services
rendered. Services I could have done at home for one quarter
the cost! But I was still covered. The expense account hadn't
run out yet. But it would the following week, and I had to
plan my first gala Christmas reception for the entire College.
That reception would take one-third of the money in the original account! All those liquid assets had evaporated with several
months to go. And my husband, so conscientious, so honest—
damn him—would insist on paying for the rest out of his own
salary. One thousand dollars. Many presidents would have let
it show up as an overrun in the budget.

Painfully, expensively, I learned that I would have to direct
and utilize a willing staff, that I could use caterers *only* for very
large functions, and that a dinner party for forty could be
cooked and served by all of us working together. That dinner
might last only three hours; the preparation for it could require
a week or more. But it could be done. And, most importantly,
I had come to realize I could do everything my way—
informally.

Since that awful first year I've managed the expense account
well. I didn't ask for an increase for six years; I've never run
out of money, and once or twice have been able to turn back
some to the College. I've also become an expert in the logistics
of entertaining. Not only are there planning, organizing, shopping, cooking, storing, seating and serving behind every enormous dinner party; there is a constant juggling of numbers,
space and material.

Odds and ends: Do we have enough candles? What's the table
linen situation? Is the silver reasonably shiny? Do we have
enough casseroles, serving dishes? What will go in what? Think
up a new idea for centerpieces. On the day of the party will
someone collect my accumulated mess of papers from the
kitchen counters, put them in a box and hide them? Will some-

one clean out the coat closet and put our coats upstairs, check the hundred light bulbs for dead ones, wipe the more noticeable finger marks off the white woodwork, put soap and clean hand towels in the bathrooms? And do we need toilet paper?

What menu? And can we afford to serve it under the fixed charge of X dollars per guest? I check my card file of every function I've ever had; have some of the guests ever had a similar meal here before?

Choose the recipes, vary the ingredients—as usual, quadruple the recipes and then explain the changes to the cook, Mrs. Allen. List when each dish should be started, how long each has to cook, and what I'll cook myself.

Write out the menu for the staff in detail. List what to do when, in what order the meal should be served and when to pour the wine. Or, if it is a buffet, draw a picture of what goes where. Type out and illustrate a menu if the meal is special, e.g., Hungarian or Middle Eastern. Have four dozen copies made. I can't do this too early, for it invariably happens that one or more recipes will have to be substituted at the last minute, because several crucial items will not be delivered to the food stores. Distributors in Boston or New York have us at their mercy.

When to shop: Frequently. Daily, if necessary. But a little energy can be conserved if the shopping is done when someone on the staff is around to carry in the groceries and put them away.

Ordering: How do I convince the milkman that an order for seven quarts of sour cream is serious? Or that I really *do* want six pounds of sweet butter? And when I have finally trained that milkman, how do I untrain him? If I want half a gallon of milk and an inadvertent slip of the pen adds a minute flag to the 1, that flag is Pavlov's bell—*seven* half gallons!

Cooking ahead: Plan what dishes can be cooked ahead. Which taste better done five days in advance, which need only two days to mellow and which have to be done at the last minute? Do I need three times the recipe for one meat dish and five times the recipe for another? Will multiplying the herbs proportionally overpower the stew? Which dish will be the most popular? If I underestimated the amount of potatoes consumed last time, will I overcompensate this time only to find a large number of dieting guests? And if they are dieting, why do I run out of salad dressing?

(Halfway to Washington, D.C.: I forgot to leave the frozen butter out to defrost. The cook is coming in tomorrow to make butter-cream frosting for four Hungarian cakes. Send an S.O.S. back to Hanover: Will someone take the butter out—quickly?)

Rewarming: How do I heat up a dinner for forty? I have two stove tops, three ovens and a warming tray. But the space is never enough. (It would be more if I could persuade Doug that the oven in the basement does not have to be used *exclusively* for baking dirt!) There are several pots of soup, three or four casseroles, three pans of potatoes to be roasted, dozens of rolls to be browned, water for coffee to be kept on a slow boil and miscellaneous other items fighting for stove space. Heat up, keep warm, serve warm. A constant battle of manipulating space and temperatures. If I heat up the casseroles first and then remove them to counter tops, freeing the stove space, will they hold their heat long enough? If I heat and serve the soup first, will I have time to warm up the casseroles before the soup is finished?

Seating arrangements: If I have forty for dinner, they have to sit somewhere. But I don't want a lot of card tables around taking up space during the cocktail hour. I'll seat the guests in two rooms—the dining room and the plant room. But if the dining table is being sat at, I will have to use the kitchen table as the buffet. Will the guests be able to go around the table without bumping into the staff or each other?

Serving: Can I serve a hot soup *and* chocolate mousse at the same party? Do I have enough bowls for both? Can I serve a salad and have enough plates to put under the dessert? "No" to both problems. The bowls and the plates will have to be whisked away, washed rapidly and reused. An assembly line of recycling.

I've done more than fifty meals of this size now. No complaints and even some compliments. But for several days afterwards I suffer from something like jet-lag. I've planned too much, expended too much. I'm red-eyed and lethargic and pooped. But there's usually not another large dinner for a while —just an airplane to catch for Kansas City.

How I envy those organized women—the ones whose wardrobes are completely coordinated, who stick to neutral shades— heather and honey—with accessories to harmonize, and whose clothes closets are so classified that they can find an entire outfit in minutes.

My closets are bulging with separates that neither mix nor match. Work around beige? *My* beiges clash. Malachite green? A daring thought. I splurge on compatible accessories—nifty accessories which are incompatible with everything else.

Not only are my clothes in confusion, my sense of style seems out of step with the fashion world. I'm neither up to the minute nor avant-garde. I'm either two years ahead or several years behind. And my budget is designed for Act III, not for Halston.

I have no trouble turning off the pathetic bleatings from *Women's Wear Daily* which sound a siren call to those lemmings called trend-setters. I deplore the initial craze. Wear Givenchy or Blass; carry Vuitton or Gucci. No need to guess the cost: It's stamped all over the damned article. Those initials are insidious. I wanted a simple white silk blouse and found one discreetly embroidered with an abstract pattern—white on white. Since I never look at labels, I could have killed Cardin, and the young woman who noticed immediately that the abstract designs on that blouse were PC's. I was a walking advertisement.

For two years I resisted von Furstenburg. She doesn't initial or sign her clothes, but the fabric, the prints, the styles are recognizable a block away. I gave in after trying on one dress, which was medium priced, comfortable, sexy and slimming.

But, of course, someone else is always wearing *my* dress at *my* party!

When John became President, I felt an expectation: "Now that you're a President's wife, who will meet and entertain the famous, you must have the appropriate clothes." If you substitute "expensive" for "appropriate," the meaning is clear.

Off I went on a buying binge with John. (I always do better when he comes along. He knows what he likes, has good taste and hides the price tags.) That spree was a disaster. Such chic outfits and all marked down. And now I know *why* they were all marked down. The whisper had gone out from the designers to Seventh Avenue to the buyers to the sales help: *"Hems will fall!"* What do you do with a number of lovely dresses and coats which, even let down and faced, are *still* too short? You hang them in the back of the closet and wait for another revolution.

Each year we are told that pant suits are out. And each year this death-knell causes panic in the north country, where winter can last two-thirds of the year. Obviously, none of those fashion dictators *ever* had frostbite. Better looking than parkas and ski pants, pant suits—the tweedy, tailored type—protect against frostbite, particularly in the knee area. Years ago, even wearing heavy stockings, my two-block walk downtown on a windy, zero-degree day was a mistake. In that temperature, flesh congeals, turns white and numb and freezes in a few minutes. My knee-caps lost all feeling for a year.

I buy many of my long dresses in the bathrobe department. Better stores label this department "hostess gowns." They are still bathrobes (nightgowns are on the next rack) or at least "lounging gowns," supposedly to be worn at home, certainly not to be seen at a formal affair. I wear these gowns to many evening functions, and have gotten away with it. In fact, a Dutch industrialist once asked me if I was wearing a Pucci. The dress did have a Pucci-type print, but since it was not a Pucci (I have never owned one and never will), had no label whatever and came from the bathrobe section, I simply smiled and said "no." If that same dress had been displayed under "evening gowns" on another floor, the price would have been double. And that doubled price would still pay for only one genuine Pucci sleeve.

I am tall for a woman—five feet eight; yet a pair of pants drags in the dirt even if I am wearing three-inch heels. Of course they drag. I am supposed to buy clogs with six-inch heels to compensate. The fact that I may break my leg, or even my neck, teetering on these dangerous stilts is irrelevant; fashion ignores medical warnings. So I have the pants shortened. But, because I am female, this is an extra charge. Any alteration on mens' suits—be it nipping here, tucking there, shortening or lengthening is included in the price. Gross discrimination! When will the feminists move in on this sexist exploitation?

Spring of 1976: I bought a dress to wear as Mother of the Bride. The belt would have to go, but something was needed at the waist. I pictured a silk flower, of watered pastels perhaps, because I would *not* be wearing a corsage. Try to buy one! Saks, Bonwit's, I. Magnin—the total number of fake flowers at all three stores could be put in a shoebox. And nothing in silk. The salespeople were snippy and sniffed, "No one is wearing them!" Spring, 1977: The scramble was on. *New York* magazine and others trumpeted, with color spreads, the marvelous new idea—the accessory of the year—fake flowers!

My hair has always been out of date. I wore my hair in a pigtail over one shoulder several years before it was in. When hair was curly, Italian style, mine was in a ponytail or a chignon; when hair was sleek and flowed around the bosom, mine was short and fluffy in front, up in the back. Then came the Hamill cut, the frizz, the frump, the punk, and I am out—again—with a wind-blown mane, which is sure to come back the day I cut my hair.

Finally, take my fur hat. When I began wearing it, no one else was. Practically nobody in this country had seen a fur hat save in pictures or films—Cossacks in caracul or Catherine the Great in sable. Mine was not nearly so glamorous. It was just a fur hat cocked over one eye. But it did cause comment. I was constantly stopped on Main Street by wags who drawled, "Is it dead? Shall I shoot it?"

People, Parties & Patter

"THE RUSSIANS ARE COMING! . . ."

The occasion was the seventh meeting of Soviet and American intellectuals and policy makers—the highest-level, non-official conference of the two countries, designed to foster mutual understanding. The first conference had been held at Dartmouth and the name became the "Dartmouth Conference," whether it was held in Kiev, in New York or somewhere in Siberia.

They came to Hanover, to our House—more than two dozen Soviet men and women: political writers, university faculty, experts on trade, experts on the United States, a former Soviet ambassador to the United Nations and translators. They were joined by their American counterparts—congressmen, industrialists, bankers, top-level professors, journalists and the directors of numerous research institutes.

In December, 1972, the Dartmouth Conference returned to Dartmouth—Dartmouth VII. I outdid myself on the reception, but I made more than my usual number of bloopers.

There was background music from a small orchestra on the landing. The landing wasn't built to hold more than two people abreast, yet four musicians managed to squeeze in music stands, chairs and themselves and to play lyrically.

The food was superb and very expensive. I splurged, since a foundation was picking up the tab, and ordered Caspian caviar —pounds of it—at $80 for 14 ounces—then! We sieved egg yolks and chopped onion; we made sizzled buttered toast squares. There was spicy salami, smoked salmon and marinated shrimp. We even managed to find three cases of the first imported Russian vodka.

Who drank the vodka and ate the iced caviar? The Americans. Who ate the marinated shrimp and downed Scotch and martinis as though the world might blow up tomorrow? The Russians. Except for one. He was true to the Soviet spirit and consumed vodka with enthusiasm. When he did the same with the caviar—two ounces at a time—I panicked, pulling the bowl away from him and clutching it to my breast. No interpreter was needed.

I listened to William Ruckelshaus (then of the Environmental Protection Agency) complain that he had tendered his resignation—as all Nixon appointees had been required to do—and that he hadn't heard yet! He would. I welcomed Donald Kendall of Pepsico, who brought me *one* bottle of his Stolitchnaya Vodka as a present. The big deal—trading Pepsi for vodka —had just gone through. Michel Friebourg, chairman of Continental Grain, soon arrived. Would that company and its deal become famous—or infamous—soon!

At the reception I asked Yuri Zhukov, *Pravda* political commentator and Deputy to the Supreme Soviet of the USSR, if he were related to the famous wartime Marshall Zhukov. He was sorry, but no. Just at that moment a young man named Gromyko passed. I turned and knowledgeably tossed out, "And you're not related to Andrei!" I turned back to Zhukov, dismissing Gromyko, and missing his answer: "As a matter of fact, I am. He's my father."

I called Morris Udall "Stewart" long before it was common— or fashionable—to do so. Seated at dinner beside David Rockefeller and Yuri Zhukov, I facetiously suggested that Russia might start becoming capitalistic by importing the Chase Manhattan. Both looked at me and roared. Chase Manhattan *was* negotiating!

We all became a little drunk, a little maudlin. Brotherhood and good fellowship—Russian and American—were flowing with the liquor.

My teenage children spent the evening scouting the translators to determine who were real, who were KGB and who were both. Amused, I mentioned this to a friend—an analyst for the CIA. He replied quite seriously, *"They* were there and most probably so were *we."* That threw me. O.K. Who among my company was from The Company?!

It began as a gesture: Let's give a victory dinner at the President's House for the 1970 football team, undefeated and Lambert Trophy (best in the East) winners. We invited the Varsity and their coaches—fifty of them—to a very filling meal. It had to be. After all, I had a rapidly growing teenage son—5'5" the year before, 6'3" now and still growing. I only had to multiply his capacity by fifty. We cooked for days: hams and baked beans, oatmeal bread and butter, salads, pecan pies with whipped cream and so much milk that I ran out of refrigerator space. Their appetites were unbelievable. After cleaning their plates, they attacked any morsel left on the serving platters. The last piece of pecan pie was auctioned off. But at least I had gauged those appetites correctly! Or so I thought, until a player quietly confided to me: "Mrs. Kemeny, we didn't want to embarrass you; so before we came over, many of us went to the dining hall for our *first* dinner."

After Ivy League football games in Hanover, we may give a cocktail party for those on the general faculty—the Medical School, Business School, Engineering School and Liberal Arts— who spent their undergraduate years at the opponent university. Dartmouth wins *more* than 50 percent of the time. Most faculty members, after spending several years at Dartmouth and teaching students on the team, begin to root for the College. There may be some twinges of divided loyalty, but usually the faculty sits on the Dartmouth side. There are always a few holdouts. Some faculty members who have been at Dartmouth for thirty years *will* wear their crimson ties to our house after the Harvard game. But that is Harvard.

When Kingman and Mary Louise Brewster visited us for the Yale game—the first time Yale had played in Hanover since the last century—Kingman did *not* wear a blue tie, and Dartmouth won. When we went down to spend a weekend with them in

New Haven, John did not wear a green tie. Yale won. It evens out.

May, 1974: John and I spent the evening with the Ted Geisels in La Jolla. He graduated from Dartmouth in 1925 and is better known by his pen name—"Dr. Seuss."

A magnificent house on a hilltop. A whimsical house with fantasy animals in oil—in every medium—hanging from the ceiling, peering over desk tops. "Cat in the Hat" cats, mystical cats, alley cats, kingly cats. I haven't had a more stimulating evening in my life. Topics ranged from the San Diego Zoo, which is a passion of the Geisels, to Nixon, who is detested passionately by all four of us.

Dr. Seuss gave me a copy of his "Marvin K. Mooney Will You Please Go Now!" inscribed: *"To Jean* (Who will change the name of Marvin K. Mooney throughout the rest of the book —I hope)—Dr. Seuss." Then in ink he crossed out the front title "Marvin K. Mooney" and wrote above: "Richard M. Nixon."

More than two months later Art Buchwald wrote a column. It began, "Washington—My good friend Dr. Seuss wrote a book a few years ago entitled 'Marvin K. Mooney Will You Please Go Now!' He sent me a copy the other day and crossed out Marvin K. Mooney and replaced it with Richard M. Nixon. It sounded like fun so I asked him if I could reprint it. . . ."

I read it, snorted and saved it. And when the Geisels visited us the next June in Hanover I confronted Dr. Seuss and waved the column at him: "I thought I was the inspiration—that you changed the title just for me!"

"Jean, I did! Our political conversation *was* the inspiration for your dedication—and then the idea was so appealing that I sent a copy *much later* to Art for his amusement."

"Dear Mr. Buchwald: Please give credit where credit is due. . . ."

June, 1974: Six weeks before the United States Supreme Court decision on the Nixon tapes. I had clipped a cartoon by Conrad showing five Justices hunched over the bench, leafing through masses of papers. One Justice says to the others, "Well, if he wouldn't pay any attention to Congress, what makes you think he'll pay any attention to us?"

Tentatively, I offered the cartoon to one of our honorary degree candidates. Would he autograph it? He studied the cartoon, chuckled and then scrawled "William O. Douglas."

The former Republican Governor of New Hampshire, Lane Dwinell, who has also held several appointed positions in Washington, was a guest for cocktails. Wire taps, electronic listening devices were dominating the news.

Governor Dwinell came up to me and remarked, relieved, "You have no bugs!"

"Bugs!" I shouted.

"Yes, plants."

Paranoid, now: "Who would want to plant bugs on us? Why would *they* tap *us?!*"

"No, no! *Bugs*—on plants—insects!"

Grant Tinker, class of 1947 and now a TV producer, returned to the College with his wife for a Q & A session with students: "Is There Life After Dartmouth?" The couple discussed careers in show business, their difficulties and rewards.

Tinker's wife is Mary Tyler Moore, a diabetic. I learned this twenty-four hours before our dinner party and, although the menu and much of the food had been prepared, I whipped up an alternate menu, just in case. "Don't worry," she laughed, "I'm a gypsy diabetic!"—and asked for a martini. The dinner? She devoured everything, including two helpings of chestnuts puréed with chocolate and sugar syrup, smothered in whipped cream. She looked extraordinarily healthy after dinner—and not a gram fatter!

In January, 1972, Robert Fish, an alumnus of the class of 1918, and a lawyer crippled since youth with arthritis, wrote his classmates a letter.

He was 75 and rather pleased to be alive. He was also pleased with Dartmouth's decision two months earlier to admit women, and he wrote his classmates why:

> . . . Best of all . . . was the decision to go coed, abandoning a position that had become increasingly anachronistic. . . .
>
> It's a decision that's temporarily painful to the men's-club mentality of superannuated alumni, but . . . Dartmouth in the future is sure to be a greater College with coeds than it could possibly be without them.
>
> Why not? As all of us know, but many still seem loath to accept, women are people, not necessarily destined to spending all their lives raising families or as housewives.
>
> Indeed, they are a most attractive people, not only in looks . . . (but in) intelligence—as they frequently demonstrate academically and by their ever-greater contributions to the arts, sciences, professions and public affairs.
>
> Not to be overlooked, either, are such civilizing qualities as compassion, kindness, sensitivity, generosity, loyalty, in which women, not men, make the best possible case for the human race.
>
> So contrary to the "he"-man who sneers them off in a recent issue of the *Alumni Magazine,* I'd be proud if Indira Gandhi and Golda Meir were Dartmouth alumnae. Naturally, I'd be delighted if the likes of Shirley MacLaine could also be claimed by the College.
>
> Come to think of it, how very nice it would be to find Shirley MacLaine at our next reunion and get her to push me in my wheelchair across that beautiful campus. That's something worth programming for our 55th in 1973. Always with the best, Bob Fish.

Quite independently, The Council on Honorary Degrees (consisting of six faculty members and the President of the senior class) had been meeting. A candidate for an honorary degree can be nominated by anyone in the Dartmouth community, with a letter stating why the nominee is deserving. These hundreds of folders are discussed by the Council individually —and secretly. And then there is a strict winnowing process until a list of about twenty candidates is agreed upon by the Council. From that list, the Trustees will pick between six and eight finalists. The Trustee choices don't become known until Commencement.

In 1973, one of the people selected—for her acting ability, her involvement with causes and her book, *Don't Fall Off the Mountain*—was Shirley MacLaine.

These two totally unrelated events—some paragraphs in a class newsletter and the choice of an honorary degree recipient —were connected by the *only* person who could tie the two events together: the wife of the Director of Public Programs was the Alumni Class Notes Editor.

Quickly she called John, who told Shirley MacLaine the story at dinner the night before Commencement. She was touched and agreed to a slight shift in the next day's formal ceremonies.

Commencement morning: The class of 1918, 55 years out of Dartmouth, marched in ahead of the academic procession to sit in a place of honor up front. Mr. Fish, who could not march, was pushed in a wheelchair by a student, and placed on the aisle.

I couldn't see Mr. Fish's face as he read the program and discovered who one of the honorary degree recipients would be. I did see it after the ceremonies—after a woman in robes and hood broke out of the solemn academic procession, went over to the old gentleman in the wheelchair and pushed him "across that beautiful campus." His face was gleaming—tears of happiness. Shirley MacLaine was crying, we all were. But it didn't end on the Green. Robert Fish and Shirley MacLaine corresponded frequently until his death at the age of 80.

When planning a party, a last-minute thought (many of mine are) may make it special. We were to give a small dinner for a retiring Trustee and his wife, who had donated a large collection of Colonial silver to the College. At the time the collection was not on public view, for security reasons. (It is now.) I went down to the vaults of the art collection and persuaded the curator to lend me what I wanted.

During dinner the conversation quite naturally gravitated to Colonial silver. I said something like, "I do admire the simplicity of Paul Revere's designs—would you care for more water?" A chortle burst from the Trustee. He recognized one of his gifts, a classic Revere pitcher, its two-centuries-old patina glowing. Most collectors would have been horrified, but not this one. "It should be *used*—not just put on display!"

The pitcher's valuation was over $20,000; I wanted to put it in the House safe overnight. My husband had a better idea: He would guard it carefully—on his bedside table. And, of course, filled with water, just in case of thirst. He poured and drank more water that evening then he ever had before or ever will.

When a dinner guest sadly tells you of the problems of a friend, a multimillionaire, you listen politely. But when you learn that the friend is broke, how do you retort? Do you nod sympathetically, or do you ask, dumbfounded, "How broke *is* broke?"

I'm blasé and sloppy about many things, but I have never forgotten one of my own parties, until recently.

Summer: the staff is on vacation; not much is going on, for a change; I haven't even looked at the calendar. John arrives home from the office, and we leisurely drink cocktails before dinner. John quite casually starts, "When my class comes over tonight. . . ." Jean, not so casually, shrieks, "*What class? Tonight!* You must be kidding—oh, my God!"

We have a little over an hour. There is nothing, really nothing, in the House to feed them, most stores are closed, I am certainly not dressed for receiving and no chairs or tables are set up downstairs! Hysterically, we leap into my Jeep and dash (if a Jeep can dash) to a country grocery that is still open. Madly, we throw cheese and crackers and beer and soda and cookies and chips and who knows what else into the cart. We overbuy and overspend, but we have the loot! Then the unloading at the front door—lugging boxes and boxes down to the basement. Six six-packs of liquid in one carton can be heavy. We race back upstairs to the kitchen for ice. Pounds and pounds of ice can also be heavy. Now to set up. Damn it! Where did Doug hide the five-foot table? Of course, in the ladies' toilet—where else? Now, where did he put the plastic trash can for ice? Never mind—we haven't time. Improvise. Heave the wood out of the brass kettle in the library. Rather a handsome receptacle for beer. I may use it again. Distribute ashtrays. Spread the cookies and crackers neatly and attractively on the trays. Why are half of the crackers broken? Spend precious minutes sorting the good from the cracked. I'm becoming cracked. Haven't time to change clothes now. At least sponge the cat hairs off my black pants. Throw a hamburger at my starving husband. We're all set and ready and it's 7:59. The first student doesn't arrive til 8:03! There was no need to hurry.

Advice: When the end of the month is upon you, *always* turn the calendar ahead to the next month. Who knows what evil lurks on the First.

It's amusing how many people feel that they must live up to an image. I had been delegated by the committee sponsoring a fund-raising gala for the arts to contact *and* persuade a famous person (voted by the committee) to make a guest (nonpaid) appearance. Telly Savalas was their choice. He was at the height of his acclaim and fame, but by a complicated series of negotiations and contacts I got the telephone number of his hotel in Berlin, where he was making a film. The first problem was timing. When would he actually be in his suite? The second was getting past the protective flunkies. I managed both of these. Savalas was worth the work, and our conversation riotous. I explained who I was—the President's wife—and that as a Columbia graduate he must know Dartmouth, that College that repeatedly beats Columbia in football. He did indeed know Dartmouth. But he did not know me, my age or what I looked like. But I was a *woman.* He was quite sure on that point. Across 4000 miles he came on strong, suave, seductive, calling me "doll," tossing endearments and regretfully turning down the invitation. He would still be filming—"But *do* call again. . . ."

Betsy Cronkite is amusing and speaks out; she was once a reporter. Walter Cronkite is warm, very informed, even nicer than one could hope and an excellent exorcist.

The four of us were sitting in the library one late afternoon about the time that there had been a new escalation of the

Vietnam War and Watergate was only a "two-bit break-in" for most people. Both the Cronkites were worried for the country.

A few weeks earlier I had learned, unhappily, that Nixon, as a young Congressman, had once stood in the doorway between the living room and the library, having been invited to speak by the faculty of the Great Issues course. Since then, each time I walked through, I mentally bumped into him. He was *always* there. How to get rid of the ghost? Cronkite! Would he exorcise the spirit? He would.

Standing in the doorway with his arms upraised, fingers in the familiar V, he announced in deep, solemn and uncanny tones, *"I am the President."* Then, with the incantation, "Out, out damned spot!" Mr. Cronkite swept away the spirit. The doorway is now clear.

Sir Georg Solti once came to dinner—a very late dinner. Georg Solti is conductor of the Chicago Symphony and Hungarian.

I had a Hungarian feast waiting for him after the concert. John says I cook these dishes better than his mother, but Sir Solti didn't know that. I had learned from a previous, sad experience as a young faculty wife that musicians are *ravenous* after a performance. Solti glanced at my exquisite buffet—*székely gulyás,* roasted potatoes, *körözött,* paprika salad and a rum cream torte—took a plate, politely helped himself to a very tiny portion of the *gulyás* and a minute portion of something else and then asked for a Scotch and soda. I was crushed.

Sir Solti tasted his portions, looked at me quizzically, finished his portions and went back for seconds. He heaped the plate.

Not shy, I asked him about the strange sequence of his eating habits. He told me: Hostesses who entertain him after a concert often cook a Hungarian meal—or what they *think* is Hungarian. But Sir Solti violently disagrees. The food is definitely *not* Hungarian. More likely it's some Slavic or, even worse, some Bulgarian mishmash. (Both inferior peoples, according to Hungarian teaching.)

The Soltis (his wife is young, beautiful and British) stayed and stayed and ate and ate. And we talked into the morning.

No tyrant, he, but a true genius, dynamic and witty, a connoisseur of women and food. Of course—a Hungarian!

In 1971 Burt Bacharach received an honorary degree, but he barely made the ceremony. Sitting up all night on a plane from California, he connected in New York with a small, slow plane which landed at our airport just in time. Whisked into Hanover, he didn't make the academic procession, but was smuggled up the back stairs to the platform. He didn't even have time to change clothes, and is probably the only honorary degree recipient ever to be hooded wearing a white turtleneck and sneakers.

In 1974 Eubie Blake, pianist, composer of songs, writer for vaudeville, Broadway and Josephine Baker was 91 going on 92. Now stooped and very old, he looked as though he might not make it through dinner. And following that meal he was scheduled to play jazz as part of a Glee Club concert. I marveled at his hands, black and gnarled and incredibly long. He did survive the dinner, but there would be that flight of stairs up to the stage! He almost skipped up those steps and gave a recital that had them stomping in the aisles. He didn't want to stop; the audience didn't want him to stop—they could have stayed all night. What keeps him alive? Music. The anticipation of music.

And most vainly I repeat the remark he made about me the next day to his luncheon partner. "She could have been in the Follies."

What a talented man! What a good eye!

It was a hectic time, but worthwhile and lots of fun. In 1971, Time, Inc., sponsored a news tour, "Report on America," for more than thirty leading businessmen of Europe, including such people as the heads of Volvo, KLM and Moet-Hennessey —and of everything else, it seemed.

A high echelon of Time–Life management: Hedley Donovan, Henry Luce III, leading correspondents and various American consultants, experts in numerous fields, traveled with the group. The purpose of the tour was "to interpret the country

at a very difficult point in American life. . . ." The businessmen from Scandinavia to Italy would learn from those at the
top the problems of a city, a campus and the government. New
York was the city. They listened to and questioned John Lind-
say, Bess Myerson, Secretary of State Rogers, Henry Ford II,
Police Commissioner Patrick Murphy and Vernon Jordan.

The campus chosen was Dartmouth.

And following the Dartmouth visit they would fly directly to
Washington for intimate meetings with Kissinger, Helms, Con-
nally, Wilbur Mills, Melvin Laird, Mansfield and Scott, and
the "loyal opposition"—Kennedy, Jackson and Humphrey.

Negotiations with Dartmouth began very early. The WATS
line hummed for months, back and forth. Schedules were drawn
to the minute. Meetings, speeches, entertainment. Where?
When? How long would each of them take? Could Mrs. Kemeny hold a reception for the group before dinner? "Of course."
Would Mrs. Kemeny hold the reception in the garden? (You're
out of your mind! A reception in the garden! In October! At
night! Iced businessmen!) "I'll try."

They arrived on a chartered Pan Am 727, hoping to land at
our airport, which is leery of jets (even Lears), since the runway
is short. Many of us went down to make sure it landed safely.
After all, if the plane crashed, the entire economy of Western
Europe might go down with it.

I gave the reception—in the garden. The weather, fickle as
always, was unusually balmy, 65 degrees, and the moon was full.
A beautiful evening made even lovelier when all the Europeans
lined up one by one and kissed my hand. The evening kept
improving. We took them to the Dartmouth Outing Club and
served a New England lobster bake. Have you ever sat at a table
with a Count, an Earl and a Sir—teaching them how to eat
steamed clams? Teaching them that tossing clam shells, dunking
and slurping is *done*. They ate a peck. And even titled persons
dribble butter down their chins.

When it was time to leave for Washington, there were under-
currents, finally voiced: "To hell with Washington. Let's stay
in Hanover!"

They'd None of Them Be Missed

THE UNPLEASANT SIDE of the job is described in this *very* short chapter. The people discussed really do exist. They'd none of them be missed, but I've got them on my list.

Fragment the fanatics (figuratively speaking). This piece could also be titled *Weather the Weatherpeople*—but I won't. (Of course, if I did, I would go on. "Storm warning: An active low front full of turbulence is moving in laden with thunder and lightning.")

Weatherpeople were the terrorist wing of the radical Students for a Democratic Society. The SDS was revolutionary, anti-establishment, but not really violent. Weatherpeople were. After their "Days of Rage" in Chicago, they surfaced on campuses, caused a few catastrophes, shattered banks and businesses and finally blew up a good portion of the leadership in their very own Greenwich Village bomb factory.

During Kent State–Cambodia, it was rumored that some had moved onto the Dartmouth campus to organize, disrupt and possibly train a few new bomb-makers. Leaflets were passed out on how to make a bomb. (I still have one; the instructions are quite simple.) The SDS was here; keeping them in check was not easy. Containing Weatherpeople could be impossible.

Forewarned is forearmed: *John stole their thunder. He coalesced all factions. He made "destruction" a dirty word on campus. The Weatherpeople, all out of wind, moved out.*

Silence the sexists. Male chauvinists come in both genders. The female of the species is pampered. She doesn't know the meaning of responsibility. She's played the game of inferiority so long that it has become fact: Men are superior in all things. She loves her lowly status. It doesn't require much thinking. "But I'm only a woman . . ." covers all contingencies.

She is a strong opponent of coeducation; women don't belong at a male institution! (Is there a hint of retroactive jealousy here? Is it a fear that if coeducation had existed in her day, competition might have been fiercer?)

She's terribly curious about my life—the inconsequential part. Heaven is going on an alumni tour. "Think of all the shopping you can do!"

She brags about her ignorance of politics and science; she's proud that her husband's profession is an enigma.

Her family has been thoroughly brainwashed: Women are inferior; women are ninnies. She's done her job; the myth has been perpetuated.

Remedy: *None. It's a waste of time to embark on a program of education. She became a lost cause at* her *mother's knee.*

How to handle a doozy. A doozy is an unforgettable, unbelievable male sexist. He's mean and usually goes after me with a vengeance. Sparks fly. Sitting beside me at dinner, he's lucky not to be skewered on my fork, for he rants: Women have no brains; women can't hold positions of responsibility; women belong in the home (chained?); his family must and does defer to his every wish; and I epitomize the worst traits of the female —outspoken, threatening, liberated, dangerous. He's real, this nasty, arrogant, crude little man.

Stratagem: *Stop sparking. Lull him into a sense of victory. Play it cool and wait, viper-like. He has a vulnerable spot—his maleness. Lash out with venom and strike that spot. Crumple him.*

Anti-toxin for anti-Semites. There's a little bit of anti-Semitism in an awful lot of people. Like syphilis it is passed down; like gonorrhea it's picked up—from some of the nicest people. Contaminated types don't break out in pustules. Nothing so overt. As always, the symptoms begin with, "Some of my best friends . . ." a cliché now, but an indication that the disease has taken hold. Would that a hypodermic could wipe out the pox in each carrier; even so, the number of ampules needed would indicate an epidemic.

I know we all meet them; I'm just convinced that I meet more—or notice more. Is there something particularly WASP-ish about me which draws the confiding, covert type into assuming that I share their prejudices? One example from too many: "Our town (a wealthy suburb) is changing for the worse. They're letting all those Jews in!"

Tactic: *Forget tact. Jab in the needle. Call them anti-Semites. Hit them with the fact that your husband is a Jew. Make them ill.*

Refuting Racism. It's not terribly chic to be a blatant racist these days. But even in the best of families runs an undercurrent: "Black is *not* beautiful." Racism is not feeling; it is whispered, but it will erupt in stress.

Our hostess at an elegant dinner party wasn't terribly chic, but she was terribly rich. She dominated the conversation from soup to dessert with one topic—the inferiority of blacks—oblivious of the fact that her staff, who had waited on us all evening, were both black.

An alumnus, an avowed liberal full of brotherly love, raged when his child was turned down at Dartmouth. His child's place *must* have been taken (usurped?) by a black! Bigots are born rapidly.

The woman, philanthropic and interesting, had a problem she shared with us. "I just can't keep a cleaning woman. The blacks, you know, all steal!"

Reflex: *There's an easy way out by placidly playing "Gentlemen's Agreement." Don't. Strike back! We did at the dinner and probably lost some donors to Dartmouth. We did with the alumnus: His second unqualified child didn't make it either. We did with the woman, but I don't think she heard.*

"Nuts" to the namecallers. It didn't happen at Bastogne: I was besieged in the back yard of a fraternity, where I fought my own battle with *a* bulge. He was a paunchy, young alumnus back for a football game besotted with bourbon and hatred for coeducation—who knows why? He fired salvos of obscenities at me—vile things about me, about John. All motion ceased; his friends were shell-shocked.

Reaction: *Curbing a wild impulse to punch his face in, I gulped several deep breaths and counted to ten—very slowly—before firing back a wounding retort. The clod! I was told I had guts by his fraternity brothers, but I wanted to belt him. If I see him again, I* will *belt him. To hell with civilized behavior.*

Understand undergraduates, even unruly ones. Usually unhappy, they must take it out on someone—frequently my husband, the "authority figure." There have been few incidents. I confiscated the billiard ball that was heaved through the hall window. I sighed, listening to the student who grabbed a mike at Dartmouth Night and then groped for an awful word to call John. The best he could come up with was "stinkpot!" His moment on stage and he blew it.

Procedure: *Find out which fraternity is missing a cue ball, but ignore the student at the mike. Venting the spleen is good for the spirit, and we still have freedom of speech at Dartmouth.*

Confront the confrontation. Start with a blistering hot day, add a gaggle of reporters, hordes of hecklers, a rabble of protesters, bewildered students, a determined President, a furious first lady. Mix them all up, and you have a sticky mess.

July's Summer Carnival is innocent fun and a fund-raising venture. The students organize it; the town supports it. There's a day-long circus atmosphere on the Green. Booths sell crafts and international food; there are a bronco-busting ride and games of chance. Money pours into the booth where stout-hearted faculty and administrators endure an eternity above a cold and deep dunking pool. "Only a quarter for three shots. Hit the target and watch the establishment splash!"

John and I had agreed to work for an hour auctioning off the services of a women's dormitory. Those services would be blown up and tagged a "slave auction" by some sexist on *The Dartmouth,* who little realized that his change of phrasing would be splashed around the world. "Slave auction!" Fighting words to feminists, who gather from miles around. "What 'slave auction'?" wail the distressed dormitory women. "What's this about a 'slave auction'?" cries UPI.

The feminists (non-students) are dishonest and sly. Cleverly, they latch onto a "repugnant event"; carefully, they avoid meeting with the Dartmouth women and discussing the situation; adroitly, however, they *do* find time to notify all wire services, *The Boston Globe* and *Newsweek* of a "media event." Where were the feminists when several deliberate sexist incidents *did* occur on campus? Noticeably absent.

The sun is brutal on the Green, and the temperature will reach 101. Only mad dogs and Englishmen go out in the noonday sun, but this is madness. All participants are ready—waiting. A reporter from *The Dartmouth* apologizes for the misrepresentation. Hisses from the feminists. John explains the situation to the large crowd, that we *will* go on with the auction and that the protest has ten minutes. Catcalls from the feminists.

After solo exhortations in which nothing of substance surfaces, they bind themselves together with paper chains simulating bondage. Then they undulate in a line, chanting and moaning their slave song. The spectacle is ludicrous. As they subside, I wonder whether the rights they respect are only their own.

Grubby and barefoot (I threw away my burning sandals), I climb on a table and begin the infamous auction. With a very large megaphone I coax out very small sums for such "demeaning" services as: typing a term paper, mowing a lawn, teaching tennis. Don't men do these things also? Sympathetic male students offer to cook dinner (if they can use Hamburger Helper) or clean an undergraduate's room. (That's a real sacrifice. Have you ever seen an undergraduate's room? Don't!)

The bids peter out; I've had to fight for each one. Sweat pours into my eyes. My voice is a croak; I'm so dehydrated I

may faint, but there's nothing to drink except pool water.
(What happened to the beer?)

The auction is finished and so am I—maybe forever. I want
to crawl to a shady spot to recover, but I'm blocked. Some
spaced-out man who hangs onto the feminist fringes harangues
me. (Stop it—I'm too hot to argue!) He *knows* how my husband
tried to sabotage the coming of coeducation to Dartmouth.
(That does it, you oaf. I'll argue! I'll demolish you!) But im-
beciles do not care about facts. Neither do the feminists, who
grab Jenny and me and spit out more accusations. Jenny is in
tears; I am frothing. To hell with skirmishes. Let's go home
and shut out the shouting.

Conclusion: *Arguing with the frenzied is useless. So is hoping
that the media will be bored. They aren't. The wires will hum
with copy. Articles quoting everybody and pictures of a scowl-
ing, frazzled presidential couple will be flashed across the conti-
nent and beyond. What unfeeling soul sent me clippings of the
whole mess from Micronesia?*

Never mind the nominee's nanny. She's really the nominee's
mother, but she's as imperious as the proverbial nanny. She
called me from a very long distance, complaining that her son's
opponent in a political race was a Dartmouth man, and that she
didn't like him. What was I going to do about it? I told her I
wasn't going to do *anything* about it.

Well . . . she would send me a book about her childhood.
(Why?) It arrived airmail, I read it, put it away and forgot it.
Out of sight, out of mind. But not for long. She called again.
Where was the book? I thought it was a present, I told her, but
it would be in the mail tomorrow (good riddance).

No . . . on second thought she'd let me keep it. But the
Dartmouth alumnus *still* had not changed his campaign! (Pour
it on, Big Green!)

Madame, I said, we will not issue executive orders regulating
the actions of alumni till death!

Resolution: *Don't answer the phone!*

The Two of Us

"But I married an instructor!" I did. And so did many other presidents' wives. Or they married struggling graduate students whose only ambition at the time was a serene life teaching in a small college.

I feel a little like the woman who marries a small-town lawyer and finds herself the wife of a member of Congress or the First Lady of the United States. At least the woman who marries a Foreign Service or management trainee *knows* her husband is reaching for the top, and frequently she is as ambitious as he.

I sympathize with those of us who were unexpectedly hurtled high alongside our husbands—who weren't prepared for a public life, who were frightened, as I was. When the decision came and my husband was chosen President, it was more than a shock. It was numbing. Plunked in a fishbowl where all could see me floundering, I was expected to cope instantly with a job for which there were no description or training, few guidelines and no aptitude tests.

No training for prospective first ladies. Yet I would have to administer, plan, speak and fund-raise, invent solutions, create new situations, constantly communicate and never stop politicking—subtly or blatantly. Obviously this would take imagination, common sense, every sense. I was expected to possess these qualities naturally and always rise to the occasion.

Something can be said for coming on the job cold or almost cold. The pressure to do it the way it was done is usually miniscule. Too much discussion, advice or how to's can really be an inhibiting factor in setting your own style and using some imagination. I do not discourage looking backwards; I *am* discouraging relying only on the methods of others. Ever-changing situations arise that need *immediate* solutions, inventive ones. If you can only mimic and rely on the past, you're dead, or, at the very least, a dud.

There are women who have married very visible men—for example, United States Senators. Yet, knowing the rigors of the job and the public exposure, they have made a constant fetish of their loathing for political life. I don't sympathize. They never tried.

There are many things one can say about being the wife of a public figure—and a university president is a very public figure. Easy, it is not! I can be very schizophrenic about my job. Who wouldn't be? It's a schizophrenic job—oscillating between periods of glamour, newness and excitement, and times of tedium and "how long can I take this!"

There is the Jean Kemeny who is warm, open and vibrant; who can see whimsy in the absurd; who is a bit of a kook (certainly unorthodox); who is impulsive and intuitive; who lacks pretense, is down to earth and witty. This part of me enjoys my own parties, is ebullient with people; wears no facade; jumps at challenges; finds satisfaction in making subtle suggestions which may have great import; loves being on stage; makes decisions rapidly; argues vehemently with anyone about anything (particularly recalcitrant alumni); meets world leaders, the great, the talented, with aplomb, ease and even sophistication; whose marriage is one of love, respect, companionship and involvement—a partnership.

There is also the Jean Kemeny who can at times be manic or lost in a black hole of depression, lazy and impatient; a bit of a hick and very naive; temperamental, brooding and bitchy. She doesn't delegate enough. She's tired of people. She's tired of talking. She's tired of thinking. She grumbles about her job. She's been on view long enough. She wants more time for herself—peace. She's past her prime and has given her best years to the College. She wants a life unfettered by continual commitment to others. But she can't even enjoy complaining! Her overactive conscience sweeps in with waves of guilt.

Some consider my job a relic from the "olden days." Since the olden days now seem to be the fifties (when I was already a full professor's wife and bringing up two children), perhaps *I* am the relic!

Less than four months after we met, John proposed and I accepted. From Europe he wrote my father a logical, well-thought-out, but very tender letter asking for my hand. He said he loved me, would try to make me happy and described our future life together: "I won't make very much money" (true); "I hope we both live a fulfilling life in an academic atmosphere" (we have); "It will be a quiet life" (false!).

Soon after we were engaged, John introduced me to Einstein. For a year John had worked with him on Unified Field Theory. Einstein, the revered master, the physicist. John, the bright, young assistant, the mathematician.

We sat in the living room of Einstein's modest house in Princeton. Still in my teens and very unknowledgeable, I was quite content to listen and say little. And then, Oh God! a phone call for John. And I was left alone with a living legend.

Stuttering, I asked advice. I was to marry a mathematician but only understood enough math to pass the College Boards. Did Einstein feel my lack of mathematical knowledge would weaken our marriage?

This very kind and wonderful man tried to reassure me. Competition in the same field, any field, *would* be detrimental. Patiently he used his valuable time to explain why. The "why" I can't remember. I was in a trance. Einstein was sitting in front of a window, the sun lighting up his hair with a halo. Mesmerized by this almost unearthly sight, I heard nothing. All that beautiful, deep philosophy is lost forever.

Absence of competition may be good, but lack of understanding is not.

I was shortchanged in high school. Women were not supposed to be interested in mathematics. (This attitude still prevails among some teachers and much of society.) After struggling with algebra, I suddenly saw its beauty, understood it and signed up to take the remaining course offered, trig and solid geometry—the only female to do so. Word spread rapidly. A confrontation with male classmates: "Don't take the course, Jean. We want to tell dirty jokes in class." Like a damn fool I yielded to peer pressure and spent that hour as the receptionist for the principal.

I wish I had had more gumption. I wish I had gone a bit further—not to compete with my husband, but to have a better understanding of the creative process, of the complex, uncharted world that utterly absorbed John for years.

But in the job we have now there's no sense of competition. There *is* intensive involvement in each other's lives. I have no difficulty understanding or empathizing. We are creating together.

A well-known feminist was horrified at the thought that when one of my ideas is used by John, he may not be able to give me credit. "But you should insist on credit, public credit!"

I will not keep a chart of those ideas of mine which have been implemented, my score versus my husband's. Unlike my feminist ally (?), I do not view married life as a war between the sexes.

Frequently John does give me the credit. I thought up a unique approach for a major fund drive. It is public knowledge. And it may work.

But it is the everyday discussions about people and policies that are hard to catalogue. I do have an impact on some decisions. I have a good intuitive feeling about people; I voice advice on problems often—very often. Some of that advice is valuable; a lot more leans toward the tyrannical.

I edit some of his papers. I can't do this for the speeches. He speaks only from notes, which drives reporters crazy. They expect advance copies—less listening, less work.

Unlike most presidents, John writes every honorary degree citation himself. He spends three or four days holed up (if he's lucky and can spare the time), immersing himself in the lives of the recipients. His citations are not rehashes of *Who's Who.* They are short and simple, amusing and personal sketches. I may be able to remember some chance remark made long before by the person who is being honored. John sometimes uses these. Occasionally, I change a word or add a phrase. One of *my* phrases was chosen by *Time* magazine in "Kudos."

I try to summarize important points I have read; I am a clipping service, and his bedside table is piled high with crudely torn-out newspaper and magazine articles which I think he should be aware of. They are crudely torn because the scissors have disappeared.

When we are on a long trip and John is driving, I read articles out loud, giving the information he will need to know at a meeting. Some are in fields I know nothing about. If they are a bit dry, such as a treatise on a model of the economy, a dramatic rendition is necessary to make them come alive—and to keep him awake.

He is probably one of the few husbands who tells his wife *everything.* So I feel I must comment on everything. I usually begin, "Well, if I were President. . . ."

Since my best and most immediate source of information about what's going on at the College is my husband, I rely on him. For hard news he's a well of information; for gossip, he's hopeless. Gossip doesn't interest him. And if by chance he *is* told some tidbit, he almost always forgets it by the time he comes home. For the juicier side of life I have to rely on other sources, which may be unreliable.

Even though he's pooped in the evening, John is patient about giving me a run-through of his day. There are times when it's rough to relive the day. A martini can be a help.

Long after he has done the run-through, long after he has filled in the details, I may think up a new and adroit question. But it is after midnight, and we have a long-standing agreement: *No* College business will be discussed after that hour.

So I try before midnight. I am apt to pounce on a disagreeable topic, rehash it and chew it to death. This is an unkind, nasty habit which I am trying to cure. (Did Jackie Kennedy ask her husband each evening during the Cuban missile crisis, "What's new in Cuba, Dear?")

John may have found the remedy.

"Tell me more about the Medical School meeting today."

My husband roars, "It's after midnight!"

"It is not! It's only ten o'clock."

"Oh, but it is—in Teheran!"

And that finishes that.

". . . Someone once asked me how I managed to sleep at night. I confessed that I had a simple secret: Each evening I told my wife all about my problems and then I slept very soundly—and she stayed awake at night. . . ." (*The First Five Years—A Report by the 13th President.*)

Ah, but I have found a solution. Closing my eyes, I can instantly become a dictator—not a benevolent one, but a despot. Rounding up those nasties—the moles who think they can build mountains, the petty intriguers and the rumor mongers, and the occasional devious, disloyal types—I pass sentence of execution. Then, with one swipe, I lop off all their heads. What a relaxing and delicious exercise!

But there are the waking hours: those days—few, it is true, but unforgettable—when everyone behaves like an idiot; when peevishness runs rampant; when small-time cliques with delusions of grandeur plot cunning capers; when radicals rant and hypocrites hyperbolize; when, no matter how hard we try, some dimwits will grumble; when it seems that it's just the two of us manning the barricades against the mob; when, by suppertime, I whole-heartedly hate the entire world. Then my husband arrives home. My husband, who has endured the same miserable day, stares at me with an expression of complete innocence and dares to complain, "Honey, it's all because of your insatiable ambition!"

I rarely criticize my husband in public; one-upmanship is not my game. On basic principles we usually agree. On the means to achieve them, we sometimes don't. But those spats can better be settled at home.

Of course, if *he* criticizes *me* in public unfairly, all rules of the game are null and void. Take a meeting at Dartmouth of New England newspaper editors. As usual, John and I were sitting at the head table. During his after-dinner speech, which shook them up with its prognostications about computer news dissemination, he shook me up by blatantly telling an untruth: "Even my wife does not read all the Sunday *New York Times!*"

Such gross misstatements must be refuted immediately, and I did—loudly! (Although I admit that I do skip portions of the classifieds and am not always current on the number of two-bedroom apartments available on the Upper West Side.)

At a stag dinner held in a function room of the Hanover Inn, the then Chairman of the Board of Trustees asked for a martini. "Make it just like the ones Mrs. Kemeny makes."

The student bartender looked bewildered and then whispered to my husband, next in line. "Sir, could you tell me how she does it?"

"Very simple—she stirs it with her finger!"

As a child I was used to clambering over shale rocks and pebbly beaches barefoot. The soles of my feet became tough, impervious to all sensation, and stayed that way. All my adolescent and adult life I've worn shoes only when absolutely necessary. And sometimes not even then.

We moved to Hanover and had two children in quick succession. When the second was born, the first was still under a year. Diapers! There were no Pampers, no diaper service and I didn't have a dryer. During the winter I had a choice: Hang the diapers down cellar where they would dry stiff as a board, or out on the line where they would freeze stiff as a board. John even caught me slogging through the snow for those diapers—barefoot.

When he became President, we each made a solemn promise to the other. John promised that I would never have to entertain a certain President of the United States, and I promised that, for his tenure, I would stop walking barefoot on Main Street.

A Saturday in February (Our day off)

Morning: I slept.
               John met with an accreditation committee reviewing a science department.
Noon: We had lunch with a new dean and his wife.
Afternoon: John graded an exam and prepared several classes for the following week.
               I made hors d'oeuvres for a very "smooth" fraternity party (75 people—3 hours work).
Evening: We were guests at a cocktail party and banquet for the student radio station. John gave a short speech.

Seven Days in May

7 consecutive days in
7 different airports in
7 different cities and
7 different hotels with
7 different beds. We did not get
7 consecutive hours of sleep.

Three Weeks (or forever) in June

I did research on honorary degree recipients and suggested phrases for the citations. I gave six receptions, one luncheon, one dinner party—all large. I appeared at one Commencement, two luncheons, five reunion cocktail parties, sat on the dais for four banquets, shook hands and talked informally to thousands.

John did a bit more: He wrote seven citations for those honorary degree recipients; he held nineteen office appointments;

he took a two-day trip to Boston and New York; he attended
twelve committee meetings; he had a luncheon with students
and held two office hours for students only; he managed to get
in six slots to catch up on the mail; in the three-day Trustees'
meeting he went to nine separate committee or full board
meetings; he attended ten receptions; at Commencement he
gave a Valedictory to the seniors and read his honorary degree
citations; he delivered seventeen separate speeches and fielded
questions from the Alumni Council, at class reunions, picnics,
cocktail parties and banquets.

He slept little.

The wife of the president of a small, very good, liberal arts college pleaded with me recently. "Please put me in the book, if
only as a footnote. Tell them that what I miss most are the rela-
tionships I had before. All the really private friendships are
gone." Mrs. James Bryant Conant agrees. "Best friends are no
longer intimate friends."

Undergoing lengthy neglect, friendships *will* be different.
But not just because of time lag. The intimacy is gone. What I
know, what's worrying me, what's about to happen, can't be
poured out to even the closest friend. Occasionally, I slip and
spew forth, letting out too much.

The easy, daily, back and forth bantering has disappeared,
for I'm lucky if I see a close friend quarterly. And then, sub-
consciously, I have to remember: "Watch it. This topic is sensitive. And that one—stay off it."

Inevitably, in an academic environment, many friends will
come from that milieu. And when your husband is President,
he holds power—jobs, tenure, firing. A friend may have a
spouse whose future depends on your husband's evaluation. No
matter how hard you try to be the same person you were before,
you won't be. The elevation makes you suspect by some; and
you may be blamed as much as your husband for any imagined
injustices.

Old friends will still be there in times of personal crisis. But
the real confiding, the uninhibited honesty, has gone.

Once—and it seems a very long time ago—going out meant relaxing. A good time to have fun and let off steam. We knew that the Presidency would change our life drastically. We were prepared for an enormous number of public appearances for the College. But we naively believed that every so often we could count on an evening out with friends, and let down. It is just not possible.

Together we go to at least one hundred outside functions a year; John will appear at many more without me. Most of these affairs are in some way official; a few are not. But at all, whether they are dreary or stimulating, the College or a related topic is the all-pervading theme of conversation.

At the nonofficial, so-called "relaxed" times, business is touched on only briefly at first. We are not questioned until a very old friend just has to bring up a gripe: "Look, I hate to bother you, but . . ." The evening deteriorates after that. One opening is all that is needed. When I, or some other sympathetic soul, tries to change the subject, someone somehow will manage to work back to a College problem.

Fed up, I went out on a limb at one party. "I'll make a bet: Pick any letter of the alphabet, common nouns beginning with that letter, and I'll prove how easily each word leads back to Dartmouth."

They opened the dictionary to "P."

Pad—dorm—housing shortage.
Pain—medical school—#1 financial problem.
Park—parking—the faculty complains.
Pea—peagreen freshmen—"My God! I forgot they are coming over tomorrow!"
Peach—fuzz—police—pot bust.
Peak—peek—honor code violation.
Pet—illegal in the dorms—including the python.
Pig—pigskin—athletics—alumni.
Pin—fraternities.
Pine—tree—symbol of Dartmouth.
Pipe—peacepipe—Indian—Indian symbol controversy.

Plunge—goes the stock market.
Pop—goes inflation.
Prune—the budget.
Pun—my husband when his job gets unbearable.

I won the bet.

The worn-out presidential couple needs TLC, intensive care. Soothing, not stimulation. Patting, not problems. Forgetfulness for a few hours.

Isolation goes with the job. People try to respect our privacy—too much sometimes. I went into the hospital for ten days with a bad back, and John continued the alumni trip without me. He came home tired and lonesome. Loads of sympathy for me poured in from friends, and I was inundated with visitors; John didn't get one invitation to have dinner—or even a drink.

Privacy is self-imposed and can be fun; isolation is neither.

We are relegated to a special niche not of our own creation. And it can be lonely up there. Surrounded by hundreds of acquaintances in the garden or chattering over a very informal dinner with visiting family, we can be isolated. The acquaintances are interested and kind; the family sympathetic and anxious to know everything. But how can you describe to anyone else the constant involvement, the facades of cheerfulness, the public scrutiny, the endless racing of the mind—even the joy, the euphoria.

An unmarried college president once remarked that the hardest part of the job, the most difficult to bear, was having *no one* to talk with completely honestly.

So we two who experience the same life are our own best friends. A cliché, trite, but oh, so true. And only with each other do we really let down, burst forth, weep, bitch, convulse in laughter or revel in the other's moment of glory.

When Reserves Run Low—Retreat

WHEN RESERVES run low, retreat. Such a sensible statement, but one we ignored for years as nonsense. Like fools, we assumed that when resuscitation was desperately needed, whirlpools of busyness would subside, a sea of appointments would part miraculously and we could slip away. We kept forgetting that the schedule had been made up a year in advance, that when we are ready to collapse, there is no block on the calendar marked "collapse."

I am now an expert on retreating. I can speak with authority on time off, getting away, vacations, unwinding and relaxing, solitude and hiding out. I have expertise on what not to do on a vacation and how to avoid the mistakes which will ruin one. I am even qualified to discuss the psychology of being sick. Priceless advice, which from time to time I follow:

Schedule Ahead

A simple-minded maxim, but not as easy as it sounds. The time to plan for a vacation is *immediately* after you have returned from one. Next time, next year seems far away when you are rested and have a vigorous I-can-take-the-world-on attitude. That vigor will evaporate rapidly. A month before vacation I am in a trance and counting down: "If I can just last through x, y and z, we leave in ninety-seven hours and twenty minutes."

You Only Live Once

We pay for all our vacations. They are not on the College's list of fringe benefits (although occasionally we combine one with an alumni tour and save the cost of the airfare). Camping would be cheaper, but as one colleague remarked, "John Kemeny's idea of roughing it is staying in a motel with only a shower." I go further. Hedonism is heaven. I want to be pampered on an island in the sun. Luxury to me is a suitcase of unread books, a warm sea, *superb* cuisine and some whistling frogs in the evening. It was not always thus. I used to resent shelling out an immense sum for a few days in the tropics when that same sum could pay for a handsome couch that would last a lifetime.

Simple axiom: No vacation = short lifetime.

Destination—Classified

Do not divulge your vacation plans. Tell the family and the office only, swear them to secrecy and plead with them to remember that their emergency may not be yours. If the news leaks out, the phone *will* ring. A network of communication blankets the world and can unearth you anywhere.

One summer a memo was sent from the President to all faculty and administrators: "We are going on ten days' vacation. I can be reached in case of an emergency. But remember, phone calls to Hawaii are expensive." We went to Etna, seven miles from Hanover. And the phone was silent.

The only problem was that we ran out of food after five days. I sneaked downtown to restock and was caught by two friends who had read the memo. The first, noticing my pallor, decided that rotten weather in Hawaii had driven us home. The second, an official at the College, worriedly rushed to the Dean. What emergency had brought us back so quickly?

Next time I'll take a sunlamp and an ample supply of frozen dinners.

When Away, Avoid People

All people. Become misanthropic. Develop a fortress mentality. Do not make new acquaintances. If you must be polite, remain anonymous. One slip and all the problems of higher education will be discussed. Piña coladas do not mix well with problems. Do not renew old friendships. An invitation to have a quiet drink will become an invitation to bring up business. Rum punches do not mix well with business.

I don't know whether daiquiris mix well with Dartmouth alumni, but martinis do. They were sent to our table by several alumni we bumped into while queuing up for a table at a Montreal restaurant. They knew we wanted to be by ourselves, waved once and sat far across the room.

A vacation isn't complete without running into an alumnus. We've met them in the elevators of almost every large city hotel we've holed up in. There was one at a reception in Barbados, one in the Bangkok airport, one by a pool in Bermuda. Almost all have antennae. They know an exhausted couple when they see one. And most have compassion. A happy greeting, a few words and they execute an about-face, leaving us alone.

Unwinding

This concept is also known as "letting down." Combine exhaustion, jet-lag, environmental and cultural shock, and you have trauma. When a psychiatrist writes that it takes three days to adjust and unwind, that a couple cannot expect to be care-free and sexy for that period, double the estimate. On an eleven-day cruise, we had a terrific last five days!

A racing brain needs time to cool down and adjust to such unnatural acts as *not* thinking, planning, creating or worrying about an imminent crisis. A tense body needs time to enjoy sleeping till noon, searching for shells and supping late.

Shopping is not relaxing! I cannot understand those vacationers who crowd the sidewalks on every island, buying, buying, buying. They are the same ones who stay up til dawn cramming frenzied motion into every minute. But how I love them when they all take off for a seven-hour trip into Caracas, leaving the entire ship to us.

We don't want to tour, we don't want to swing, we don't want to *see* . . . except for the zoos. I'd walk a mile for a camel.

How to Really Relax

Discuss four topics only: sun, sea, sex and "When do we eat next?" Forget the outside world. Do not mention a College called Dartmouth. Stop believing that *The New York Times* is the only reason for living.

I used to be the villain on vacation. The day was not complete without an hourly summary of the news. If I couldn't get the airmail edition of *The Times,* for which I would pay an outrageous sum, I sulked. The one vacation which cut us off completely was idyllic—so, of course, I vowed that no news was good news. But I lapsed in Hawaii, 5000 miles from Hanover. A paradise of curving beaches, palm trees and snow-capped volcanos. Breakfast on a sunny balcony amidst a wild profusion of bougainvillea. Tiny birds begged for crumbs. The sun was healing—strong and hot. So was the coffee. But I *had* to have something to read with that coffee, so I cheated and asked for the provincial newspaper. What's doing in Hilo? Not much. But in other news: a basketball coach's flirtation with another job. His present job? Coach at Dartmouth College, Hanover, N.H.!

Hiding Out—in Bed

I begin by shouting: "Oh, to be Vegetable for a Day!" (I've been "Queen . . .") That idea expands into the blissful thought of languishing in bed for a week, feeling fine. Delightful! No responsibilities, no guilt, a superb menu thought up by someone else and a pile of trashy thrillers on the bedside table. Rather like a short convalescence from TB without the disease.

Then my overactive New England conscience intrudes: "Not only do you have no time to be well in bed, you have no time to be sick there. You have to arrange the student initiation into Phi Beta Kappa, followed by a cocktail party and a dinner for Robert Frost's former secretary, and then fly off to Philadelphia, where John will receive an honorary degree from the University of Pennsylvania. You cannot cancel!" Shrug off the ache, forget bed and plod on. A martyr? So much the better! And if your physician says that trying to keep you in bed is like containing Hurricane Edna in the cellar, ignore him.

So when the flu strikes periodically with great vengeance, I drag on—grouchy, snuffling and dripping. Aspirin, plenty of liquids and bed rest are prescribed. "Bed rest!" I howl. "*When!*" Not until I am nasty to all, consumed by that evil, rotten feeling and unable to walk or breathe do I obey my husband's bellow, "*Go to bed!*" And there I stew, obsessed by things undone. I cannot languish lengthily, I'm too sick to enjoy it; food is noxious; I can't keep my mind on my thriller; the sheets are littered with Kleenex; TV is inane and sneaking a cigarette is no fun. A few puffs and my lungs rebel—as lungs should with double pneumonia. Two weeks in the hospital. "Calvinism carried too far," snorts my physician.

A Retreat of One's Own

We had to get away from the President's House, with its ringing telephones and reminders in every room of work that should be done. We had to escape from the active, alive campus outside the front door. We needed a place to hide. Yet we were limited by sparse and unpredictable time off. No trekking to remote lakes, no hours of driving to get there. We needed a complete change of scene, a place to forget—but close to town.

The plan seemed simple at first. Buy land, build a small retreat (put equity into something and save the cost of some vacations) and then use it as a permanent home after the Presidency. All this had to be in Hanover, not just because we love it, but —just as important—because I can't bear to give up my voting registration!

Two parcels of land were available, hilltops with spectacular sixty-mile views to the Adirondacks. Each fell through, the first because the price tripled in a year, the second because the unsympathetic State of New Hampshire flatly refused to approve our proposed, well-engineered and very expensive leaching field. (Unless, of course, we would do without flush toilets, a garbage disposal, washing machine and a dishwasher!)

Meanwhile building costs kept pace with the speed of light. Building even a modest dream house from scratch would put us in hock forever. My minimum space requirements for storage were unaffordable at $40 a square foot. (I collect things!)

John brilliantly suggested we change tactics. Search for land already built on. "But don't buy the first place you see." We didn't. We bought the second.

"Less Than Forty-five Minutes from Broadway," or forty minutes from Webster Avenue, we found a prize—a simple ranch perched on a hill. Inside, a mammoth fieldstone fireplace built with love *and* skill (it draws); a polished oak floor in the sunny living–dining room; *lots and lots* of storage space. Outside, a deck inundated with birds and mammals, a panoramic view of the Vermont mountains, ten sloping acres and blessed quiet.

We can dash up for dinner, spend a day and a night, or sometimes a week, if we have one.

In every new city I always do the telephone book: A glance at the front page for a brief history of the area; a glimpse of the Yellow Pages for services available, and those that are not. On a vacation in Bermuda, between sunning and gluttony I culled cottage names, searching for an inspiration for our new retreat.

Tranquil names: Escape, Felicity Hall, Happy Here, The Cocoon. Silly names: Rock Bottom, Mushroom Cottage, Oleander Corners, Onion Patch. Classics: YooHoo, Wimple-Up, Timberdoodle-Too.

I was not inspired. I came up with awful titles like Vermont Vista, Hemlock Haven and Civilization Copout.

When Franklin Roosevelt called his retreat "Shangri-la," it suggested a place of peace. But Eisenhower, devoid of poetic imagery, changed the lovely name to "Camp David," evoking at best a blank—or at worst a grandchild. Who wants a grandchild at a retreat?

Our house needed a classy designation, a name that would enshrine it, or at least be unforgettable.

My mind was blank, my imagination dry until the day we watched the antics of a crazy bird with an upside-down view of the world. NUTHATCH! No one forgets the name of our retreat *now*, except for a certain Dartmouth vice president who still has trouble: "When are you going up to 'Boobyhatch'?"

"Nuthatch" is off Dogford Road, a meandering thoroughfare. According to legend, it was so named when everyone living on it had both a dog and a Ford.

The bird-feeder is well stocked with sunflower seeds all year, including Summers. The Audubon Society gasps: "You are upsetting the balance of nature!" How about our balance? The variety of visitors lured to the deck is mind-boggling and mind-resting. Who thinks about problems when the Red Baron and some of his squadron swoop in at night? Flying squirrels are rarely seen and harder to photograph, say books on mammals. Ours are tame enough to let me take their picture with a flash from two feet away.

The bird feeders are a magnet for over thirty varieties of birds, squirrels, field mice and chipmunks. That large furry teddybear, sleeping in the feeder, was the first of twenty-two raccoons. All are named, all recognized now. They climb up a sixteen-foot piling, maneuver over a three-foot overhang and bounce onto the deck. Moshe (Dayan) was the sleepy one, sweet and gentle. *He* became a *she* when she brought her baby, Shalom. The parade has never stopped. My favorite is Bagel's baby, Cream Cheese, a loveable, tiny blob in July—a thirty-pound mush in November. He sits in my lap and lets me pull his tail.

We feed them occasional bits of veal marsala, grape jelly, bananas and cookies, lots of baked custard (raccoon-style—with less sugar) and pounds of dog-kibble. Nightly they also devour a gross of leftover rolls which the dining hall would otherwise throw away. Freshly shucked sweet corn is ignored!

The birdbath is used occasionally by birds and squirrels and constantly by raccoons. They drink from it, sit in it, roll their rolls in it, wash all four feet in it.

New Hampshire is Ice-Age country. Picturesque hunks of sculptured glacial boulders are scattered on everybody's property but mine. I wanted one rock—a pet rock—but not the tiny boxed one from Bloomingdale's. I asked a construction firm dredging a pond nearby to bring me the largest hunk their truck could carry, after one of the crew and I had squished barefooted through mud flats selecting possibilities. The rock was more expensive than Bloomingdale's—a yard high and five feet long with rounded contours, pleasing to the eye. With a little imagination it almost resembled Snoopy.

With a little ingenuity, the rock *became* Snoopy. Black contact paper made an ear eighteen inches long, an eye, an eyebrow and a round nose four inches in diameter, which I stuck to the pitted granite. The nose is of particular interest to small animals. It disappears periodically. But I usually find it within a radius of fifty feet, where it has been dragged, sniffed at, found inedible and discarded.

Solitude

(Also called privacy or "all alone with no telephone.") People disagree on their need for privacy. John and I differ on the meaning. He defines solitude as being alone with me. *I* define it as being alone with me.

I need time by myself. Nuthatch becomes a retreat, a place to rest and regroup. I am not tied to a schedule. I frequently do little that in tangible terms could be called constructive.

Sometimes I write, but more often I muse, staring off at the Vermont hills, day-dreaming.

Spending an hour waiting for the first raccoon to climb up on the deck, or three hours waiting for the resident red fox to trot by, is not wasted time. It is healing time.

I talk to the animals. They may answer with trills and chirps and snorts, but the language isn't human. I don't need newspapers when there's a bit of the world going on outside my window. But it's not a people world. The only hint of violence is the red squirrel chasing the gray squirrel. I can wake when I want to, take six naps a day or not go to bed at all. I may have dinner in the afternoon, dinner at midnight or no dinner at all.

A little freedom can banish that locked-in feeling. A little convalescense is vital, for vitality is the essense of my job.

What a Life!

MOST OF this book has been about my role at Dartmouth. I have tried not to bore the reader with a litany of childhood remembrances. And I have compressed my first forty years. But the real me would be missing if I neglected to relate a few incidents from those four decades: I walked *down* the Washington Monument; I rode a pregnant elephant bareback near the Cambodian border (thin pants, thick bristles); I protested against George Wallace; I slid down an 8000-foot mountain in the Austrian Alps on my fanny; I was a waitress in a Summer hotel and spilled an entire tray of food on the heads of the owners; I had a pet monkey whose only fault was to have diarrhea on guests; and I started a chain of events which ended in Watergate (but that is another story).

I am speculating about further fascinating things to do after John resigns the Presidency, but for these you'll have to wait til the end of the chapter.

Uneducated and ignorant, I founded a new school in 1970—a school for one presidential wife. I wrote the primers, devised the curriculum and taught the courses to myself. I determined what questions to ask and mastered some of the answers. This book is my thesis, written under an adviser—me. When I graduate, it may not be with honors, but my grade should be more than a gentlewomanly C+.

One-fifth of my life has been spent in this job. In any life there are good times and bad times. As the President's wife, the peaks seem higher, the valleys deeper.

I hate paragons—possibly because I am not one. Besides, paragons are saints, and saints are martyrs, and martyrs are bores. Being less than a paragon is a very human condition, and imperfect people can complain. I do. My grumbles and complaints are bared below. But imperfect people can also rise to new heights. Paragons can't; they're already there. Imperfect people can look up, learn and live a rewarding life. I have. My great satisfactions follow the grumbles.

There are:

The exhausting times

When, after never-ending hecticness, I moan, "For what? Does all the work we put into this job make any difference?"

When the cumulative wear and tear shows up in short tempers, baggy eyes and sleep-walking actions.

When that article on the bedroom floor that I have tripped over for a week stays there; bending down to pick it up and put it away is too much effort; and anyway I don't know where to put it. My filing system broke down years ago.

The "I hate people" times

When one nasty incident cancels out the nine nice ones that happened the same day.

When I have to deal with churlish alumni or childish students. (The adjectives can be reversed.)

The dull times

When I tot up all the data I have to absorb, store it and spit it out on cue.

When documentation (pure bureaucracy!) must be kept up to the minute.

When the same problems keep popping up, disguised ever so slightly, and the same arguments won't die.

When the years take on a frightening similarity and planning
becomes a chore, a trauma.

When that once-fresh and innovative imagination has worn
down and becomes sluggish.

The shrewish times

When I unearth "the no-escape clause" in an unofficial contract.

The banshee screeching times

When John must listen to my cacophonic cries: *"I can't shake
2000 hands tonight. I can't stand up!"* . . . *"Describe June to
me. I seem to remember it was a lovely month. But I've lost it
ten years running!"* . . . *"I don't give a damn who they are. I
won't plan one more dinner party!"* . . . *"You mean we've got
to travel again? I haven't unpacked from last week's trip!"* . . .
*"Another dedication tomorrow? Will the building really miss
me?"*

But . . .

I'm not on stage every minute. It just seems so.

I haven't "sacrificed everything for my husband's career." If I
wail that life is dull, dull, dull, I remember my old life of dab-
bling, which was a lot duller.

I've uncovered talents that surprise me. I thought my mind
was sloppy, but I discovered a logical and incisive one. Under
pressure, I can organize and plan, make snap decisions—good
ones—and contribute ideas that have been implemented as College policy.

I found energy in some hidden reservoir. Always a late bloomer,
I might never have budded. I've grown in the job *because* of

the job. I can argue issues with less heat and more force; I see through a fog of rhetoric to the nub of a problem.

Emotionally, I've matured. (If a woman in her late forties is allowed to mature. Physically, please let me regress ten years!) I have created a unique position at a unique institution. I am listened to and utilized (sometimes too often!)—an unknown who became a bonus.

The Presidency has certainly strengthened our marriage. Sharing common problems day and night will either make or break one. John is married to me first; his job comes second. We complement each other. The best of both of us makes a terrific team.

My husband is a remarkable man—one who has changed the face of education; who was called "the best university president in the country" by the editor of one of the finest metropolitan newspapers. But his job would be unbearable alone. I have an obligation that goes beyond this era's freedom of choice. I have to and I want to support this man of enormous talent, who might function badly without me.

If I had to entertain every day, I'd smash the china. If the line I was expected to walk remained too narrowly defined, I'd stumble and fall on my face. If I couldn't speak out on issues, I'd scream. If there weren't periods of solitude, I'd fracture the fishbowl. If I couldn't be me, I'd go bonkers.

The bonds are still there, but I've loosened them. Protocol is only a shadow. I've broadened that narrow line. I've established my own style, and I've done it my way.

Still, there *are* those days when I swear I'll never plan another party, take another plane, make another list, think up another response. Days when I want to get the hell out, to be a "free spirit" without embarrassing my husband or Dartmouth. In trying times such as these, I put into use that very useful slogan: "Put off till tomorrow what you can't face today."

I am the masochistic type who read *Fail Safe* during the Cuban missile crisis, *The Ghost of Flight 401* on an airplane and *First You Cry* when they discovered a lump a couple of years ago. I was the blasé type who couldn't have a biopsy until

Monday because, "It's the Harvard weekend and I'm swamped!" I was the courageous type who had cancer and a radical mastectomy and didn't cry. I was "a gallant lady" who held up for six months before collapsing and admitting that the specter of dying too soon was terrifying. And I became the selfish type who wanted time to create tangible, lasting things, who bitterly resented giving that precious time to Dartmouth. Most of the fear and much of the resentment has faded. But when I feel sorry for myself or a bit fearful about the future, I try to remember a pungent inscription Archibald Macleish wrote to me years ago in a book of poetry: "For Jean, who *is*."

"Is" is today. There's a new crop of students arriving, new cities to visit, new people to meet, a new crisis to head off. So I plunge in again with my 70th wind, knowing I *have* made a difference, tangible and lasting.

And there is a future. There has to be. Think of the fascinating experiences I've yet to have. I want to go on a long-term archeological dig; hang the expense and eat lobster for a month —at breakfast, lunch and dinner; write a novel of medical detection; just *once* ski down a slope without leaning into the hill; try to paint again; hear communications from intelligent beings in outer space and understand the language of dolphins; have carte blanche at the bookstore; own a tiger cub which will never grow up; learn *not* to be intimidated by New York City; and walk *up* the Washington Monument.

Epilogue

THE FINAL DRAFT of this book was nearly done when John handed me a thick, creamy envelope with "Office of the President" discreetly engraved in the corner and "For the epilogue" penned across the center. Inside was a letter and an enclosure:

To the First Lady from the President:

Recognition long overdue!

John.

The enclosure? One green plastic card with raised gold letters:

JEAN A. KEMENY
FIRST LADY

A Dartmouth College ID card! I am *official*.

DARTMOUTH COLLEGE

HANOVER
NEW HAMPSHIRE

This map is not drawn to scale but has been deliberately distorted to accentuate certain features.

For general reference, the East-West distance across the Green is about 100 yards.

VOX CLAMANTIS IN DESERTO

1769

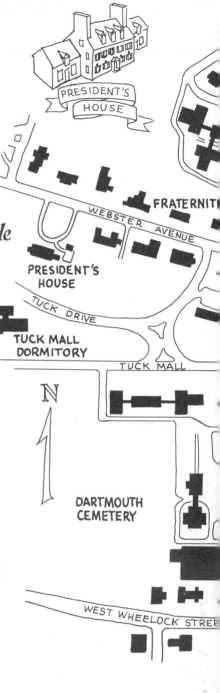

PRESIDENT'S HOUSE

FRATERNIT

WEBSTER AVENUE

PRESIDENT'S HOUSE

TUCK DRIVE

TUCK MALL DORMITORY

TUCK MALL

N

DARTMOUTH CEMETERY

WEST WHEELOCK STREE